WORLD WRITERS

Real Courage:
The Story of
Harper Lee

WORLD WRITERS

Real Courage:
The Story of
Harper Lee

by Katherine Don

MORGAN REYNOLDS
PUBLISHING

Greensboro, North Carolina

For my late grandfather Ronald B. Gilbert,
a true Atticus of our time,
who fought for civil rights,
followed his compass,
and kept his eye upon the donut

TO KILL A Mockingbird

A NOVEL BY

HARPER LEE

World Writers Series

Best of Times: The Story of Charles Dickens

Ralph Ellison: Author of Invisible Man

England's Jane: The Story of Jane Austen

Savage Satire: The Story of Jonathan Swift

Writing is My Business: The Story of O. Henry

Gift of Imagination: The Story of Roald Dahl

Deep Woods: The Story of Robert Frost

Tortured Noble: The Story of Leo Tolstoy

Rhythm and Folklore: The Story of Zora Neale Hurston

A Great and Sublime Fool: The Story of Mark Twain

Strange Creatures: The Story of Mary Shelley

C. S. Lewis: Twentieth Century Pilgrim

Self-Reliance: The Story of Ralph Waldo Emerson

From China to America: The Story of Amy Tan

Be Not Afraid of Greatness: The Story of William Shakespeare

Poetry Came in Search of Me: The Story of Pablo Neruda

Suzanne Collins

Rick Riordan

Real Courage: The Story of Harper Lee

Real Courage: The Story of Harper Lee
Copyright © 2013 by Morgan Reynolds Publishing

Library of Congress Cataloging-in-Publication Data

Don, Katherine.
Real courage : the story of Harper Lee / by Katherine Don. -- 1st ed.
    p. cm.
Includes bibliographical references and index.
ISBN 978-1-59935-348-7 -- ISBN 978-1-59935-349-4 (e-book) 1. Lee,
Harper--Juvenile literature. 2. Authors, American--20th
century--Biography--Juvenile literature. I. Title.
PS3562.E353Z59 2013
813'.54--dc23
[B]
                                   2012016871

Printed in the United States of America
First Edition

Book cover and interior designed by:
Ed Morgan, navyblue design studio
Greensboro, NC

TABLE OF CONTENTS

The Old Courthouse Museum,
Monroeville, Alabama

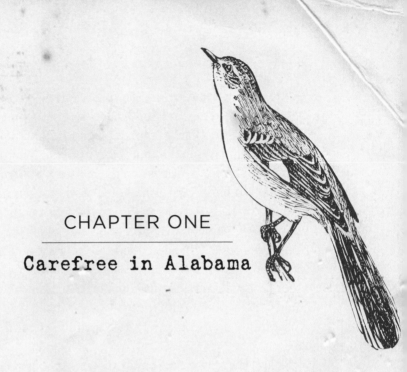

CHAPTER ONE

Carefree in Alabama

In 1964, when Nelle Harper Lee was thirty-eight years old, she was one of the most famous writers in the world. Her first book, *To Kill a Mockingbird,* won the Pulitzer Prize in 1961, and in 1962, its film adaptation won three Academy Awards. Everybody wanted a piece of her. She spent her days sifting through fan mail, talking on the phone, and assuring friends, family, and fans that her second book would soon be finished.

Nelle Harper disliked the attention. Her older sister, Alice, later said that in these early days of fame, "There were so many demands made on her. People wanted her to speak to groups. She was terrified of speaking." To make matters worse, her hometown of Monroeville was the inspiration for Maycomb, Alabama, the setting of *To Kill a Mockingbird.* Some were angry that Nelle used real people and stories to populate her fictional world. One family even threatened to sue because they believed their son was the inspiration behind Boo Radley, the town recluse in *To Kill a Mockingbird.*

Nelle couldn't find peace or privacy anywhere. "I have about 300 personal friends who keep dropping in for a cup of coffee," she complained to a friend. "I've tried getting up at 6, but then all the 6 o'clock risers congregate." Meanwhile, national events drew attention to Nelle's book, which included stories about racial injustice. America was entangled in the tensions of the civil rights movement: desegregation was underway, Dr. Martin Luther King Jr. called for equality, and the Civil Rights Act of 1964 banned discrimination based on race, color, religion, or national origin. Everybody wanted Nelle's opinion on these issues, but she was a novelist, not a politician, and she began to resent their questions.

In 1964, she spoke on a radio show with journalist Roy Newquist, who asked about her aspirations as a writer. In response, Nelle revealed her most cherished ambitions:

> I hope to goodness that every novel I do gets better and better, not worse and worse. I would like, however, to do one thing, and I've never spoken much about it because it's such a personal thing. I would like to leave some record of the kind of life that existed in a very small world. I hope to do this in several novels—to chronicle something that seems to be very quickly going down the drain. . . . As you know, the South is still made up of thousands of tiny towns. There is a very definite social pattern in these towns that fascinates me. I think it is a rich social pattern. I would simply like to put down all I know about this because I believe that there is something universal in this little world, something decent to be said for it, and something to lament in its passing.

This was Nelle's last extensive interview. She never wrote another book, and she stopped speaking with journalists. Today, at eighty-six years old, she resides in a nursing home in Monroeville. Many consider her to be one of the most persistent mysteries in the history of literature. How could somebody write a Pulitzer Prize-winning book and then disappear? To understand the answer to this question, look no further than Nelle's idyllic girlhood, in which she played, laughed, and lived in a very small world.

Nelle Harper Lee (pronounced "Nail Harpuh" in Alabama) was born on April 28, 1926, in Monroeville, Alabama, the youngest of four children. Her older brother, Edwin, was six years her senior; her sister, Louise, was ten years older and already in high school when Nelle was little, and Nelle's oldest sister, Alice, was fifteen years older. Alice left for college when Nelle was very young but returned one year later and stayed home until 1937, when Nelle was eleven.

The Lee siblings had affectionate nicknames for one another. Nelle was "Dody," Edwin was "Brother," Louise was "Weezy," and big sister Alice was "Bear." Alice later said that since they were so far apart in age, it was almost as if each was an only child: "We were not companions for each other until we were adults."

Nelle's father, Amasa Coleman "A. C." Lee, was a leading citizen in Monroeville. He was a representative in the Alabama legislature, director of the Monroe County Bank, a lawyer, and part owner of the local newspaper, the *Monroe Journal*, since 1929. A. C.— "Coley" as a child—was born in the rural village of Georgiana, Alabama, in 1880, a middle child in a large family of nine, two of whom died in childhood. The family moved to rural Florida when Coley was a toddler, and every Sunday, his parents took him and his siblings to a Methodist church,

a three-mile ride from the family farm. They believed in the teachings of Methodism, which emphasized the importance of education, social service, and personal responsibility in living a moral life.

Coley had only one year of formal education, but he loved to read from an early age. In the late nineteenth century, farmers moved their families to wherever the best and cheapest land could be found, so children oftentimes attended rural schools for a short time, only to pick up and move to a new farm. Parents who could read and write taught the skill to their children.

When he was sixteen, Coley taught school for three years in Florida. At nineteen, now calling himself A. C. Lee, he moved to Monroe County in southern Alabama, where he became a bookkeeper. In 1910, at age thirty, A. C. married Frances Finch. They had been introduced to one another at church. Frances, Nelle Harper's mother, was born in Monroe County in 1888. Her father, James Cunningham Finch, grew up on a farm in Alabama, and her mother, Ellen Williams, grew up on a large plantation between Mobile and Montgomery that bordered the Alabama River and undulated with rolling waves of pine-dotted hills. Before the Civil War, slaves on the Williams plantation hauled loads of cotton onto steamboats that carried the bounty along the Alabama River, which connected the timber and cotton port towns of southern and central Alabama.

When Frances was fifteen, her parents sent her to the progressive Alabama Girls' Industrial School, where young women learned reading, writing, and arithmetic in addition to the traditionally feminine arts of cooking, sewing, home nursing, typewriting, and painting. Frances was a pianist and vocalist in school productions.

In 1913, Frances and A. C. moved to Monroeville, population seven hundred, a tiny, landlocked town that a passing confederate soldier had once deemed the "most boring place in the world." Before automobiles, it was a treacherous journey from Monroeville to larger towns like Mobile to the south or Montgomery to the north. It was surrounded by hills of red clay, patches of pine forest, and cotton fields; by 1913, a railroad stop connected Monroeville with larger towns. The local sawmills, lumber yards, and cotton ginneries produced lumber and cotton for trade. As the town's population grew, a business class of merchants, lawyers, bankers, and store owners emerged—A. C. became the financial manager at Bugg and Barnett, the local law firm. In 1915, A. C. passed the bar examination, and Bugg and Barnett became Bugg, Barnett, & Lee. By the time Nelle was born, her family was one of the most reputable of Monroeville.

One of many historic buildings in Monroeville

From an early age, Nelle was a tomboy. She had short, straight chestnut brown hair, wore coveralls whenever possible, and absolutely despised socks. She had a quick temper, liked to fight, and courageously explored Monroeville and the surrounding pine forests, swimming creeks, and farmlands. She lived in a big white bungalow on South Alabama Avenue, a treelined street two blocks from town square, where passers-by marveled at the Monroe Courthouse, the pride of Monroe County. It was a four-story red brick structure topped with a white, ornate clock tower that boasted four clocks, one facing each side of the square. In the lawn surrounding the courthouse, men congregated to talk business or play checkers. The *Monroe Journal* called the courthouse interior "one of the handsomest and most conveniently appointed in the state."

Monroeville had a bank, a furniture store, a cotton warehouse, three pharmacies, and shops providing hardware parts and dry goods. M. Katz's department store contained a fabulous assortment of gifts, clothing, and children's toys. Gus Barnett, owner of the hardware store, had a wooden leg that was a source of endless fascination for little kids like Nelle. In the 1930s, the streets of Monroeville were unpaved, and horses galloped into town, kicking up swirls of red dust. Some families, including Nelle's, already owned an automobile, but horse-hitching rails stood outside the courthouse. The cotton ginnery was two blocks from town, and mule-drawn wagons carried cotton in from the country. At noon, the saw whistle blew, alerting women within hearing distance that it was time to serve dinner, the midday meal. Nobody in Monroeville locked their doors, and most everyone went to church—Baptist or Methodist. In the afternoons, ladies gossiped on porch swings or brought homemade food to whoever in town was ill that day.

While A. C. worked in his law office above the bank in town square, Nelle roamed free with her best friend, Truman Streckfus Persons, a tiny runt of a boy with a fierce personality who moved into the house next door when he was three and Nelle was two. They were precocious, imaginative children—they dueled in fake sword fights, battled imagined armies of giant lizards, and pretended they were Creek Indians, Sherlock Holmes, Dr. Watson, or other characters from their favorite books. Sometimes Nelle's brother Edwin, who loved books, read out loud to them.

When Nelle started the first grade at Monroeville Elementary School, she became Truman's protector, since he was a mischievous coward who despised violence yet provoked his schoolmates. Truman was deeply sensitive: sometimes, he angered folks just to test out whether they liked him. One morning, they departed for school through Nelle's backyard, which bordered the elementary schoolyard. They passed a sand-bed under a big oak tree that was called the "Kitchen." According to a popular game, any boy who walked through the kitchen would be attacked. "Hot grease in the kitchen, go round, go round!" was the alarm call. On that morning, Truman walked right into the kitchen, and was immediately pummeled by his schoolmate, the King of the Kitchen. Nelle jumped into the group of boys, pushing and shoving her way to Truman. "Get offa him!" she yelled as she pulled him to his feet.

This wasn't her first fight, and it wouldn't be her last. One day, during a school dodgeball game, she punched a boy in the stomach after he pulled her hair. When his friends came along to help, she beat them up, too. Depending on who you talked to, Nelle was either queen of the tomboys or a big bully. She was fast to fight, but was also kind, sensitive, and fiercely loyal. Up until junior high, she regularly played football and baseball with the boys.

The connection between Nelle and Truman went deeper than schoolyard scuffles. By the age of six, they were both budding writers. The character Dill in *To Kill a Mockingbird* is based on Truman, who grew up to be Truman Capote, the famous writer. In her book, Nelle describes Dill in detail: "He wore blue linen shorts that buttoned to his shirt, his hair was snow white and stuck to his head like duck-fluff; he was a year my senior but I towered over him. . . . we came to know Dill as a pocket Merlin, whose head teemed with eccentric plans, strange longings, and quaint fancies." When Truman moved to Monroeville, he was "like a bird of paradise among a flock of crows," according to one of his elementary school teachers. Whereas many of his classmates lived on farms and didn't wear shoes to school, Truman wore clothing from fancy department stores. He spoke in a high-pitched voice, and moreover, he had a high vocabulary and used strange words that the other children didn't recognize.

"He wore blue linen shorts that buttoned to his shirt, his hair was snow white and stuck to his head like duck-fluff; he was a year my senior but I towered over him. . . ."

His family life was a source of gossip: Truman's parents, Lillie Mae Faulk and Archulus Julius Persons, had divorced after a tumultuous marriage, and Lillie abandoned little Truman to her cousins at the Faulk household, which consisted of Jennie, Callie, Bud, and Sook, four unmarried siblings who lived next door to Nelle on South Alabama Avenue. Aunt Jennie and Callie owned a millinery shop in town. Jennie, the strict head of the household, scolded Truman with frequency. Sook, a gentle, childlike woman who never left the house, was beloved by Truman, Nelle, and "Big Boy" Jennings Faulk Carter, Truman's cousin. After church on Sundays, they crawled into Sook's lap on the back porch and read the funny strips from the *Monroe Journal* while the adults ate teacakes and drank coffee in the kitchen.

Nelle, Truman, and Big Boy gossiped about the strange characters of South Alabama Avenue. Two doors down was a deteriorating house with peeled, sunbaked paint and a ramshackle backyard. Inside lived the Boleware family: Alfred Boleware, his wife Annie, two grown daughters, and Alfred Jr. "Sonny" Boleware, the mysterious young man who, according to town gossip, was homebound since 1928. As a teenager, he had stolen from a local drugstore. The two other teenaged culprits were sent to a state industrial school, but Alfred insisted that Sonny be left in his custody. When Nelle and Truman were children, Sonny rarely left the house. Sometimes, he was seen on the front porch at dusk.

As years went by, the legends escalated. Children said the Boleware house emanated evil vapors and attracted ghosts and other spirits. They whispered that if Sonny ever got out, he would stab neighborhood kids with a butcher knife. According to Charles Ray Skinnner, a friend of Nelle's family, "Mr. Boleware ruined his son's life . . . The man was *mean.*" Sonny died of tuberculosis in 1952. His gravestone reads, "To live in the hearts we leave behind is not to die." Truman later said it's "absolutely true" that Sonny was the inspiration for Boo Radley.

Across the street from the Bolewares' lived Mr. and Mrs. Ralls, who ran a boardinghouse that hosted an ever-rotating cast of eccentrics for the children to spy on. Their kitchen was a popular destination for Nelle and her friends. Big Boy later recalled the wonderful foods they encountered there: "Mrs. Ralls . . . cooked three big meals a day for her boarders and for the traveling salesmen who stopped there to eat. She kept fruit and custard pies, pound cakes, and sugar cookies on hand and readily offered these to us when we stopped in for a visit." Another adult friend was Anna Stabler, who lived in a shack behind the Faulk house. Said to be the daughter of a white judge and a Negro maid, her father had insisted that she live in the white part of town rather than in Clausell, where all the black folks lived. Anna drank a lot, played the fiddle, and loved to sing.

A 1934 photograph of an old house in Monroeville, Alabama

In 1932, Truman's mother, who had been living in New York City, remarried to a man named Joe Capote. She decided that Truman, now eight years old, should join her and his stepfather in New York. Upon receiving this news, Truman cried and cried, and then decided to throw the biggest party Monroeville had ever known. It would be a Halloween costume party, and Truman himself would award the prizes. Nelle borrowed Edwin's air rifle for a balloon shooting contest. Aunt Jennie even consented to holding it on a Friday night, which was unheard of in Monroeville because parents from the country had to ride their children all the way into town. For this reason, the party would be for adults, too.

As Truman, Nelle, and Big Boy put a guest list together, Truman insisted on inviting John White, a black man who helped Truman's cousin with chores. Nelle, in turn, insisted they invite Sonny Boleware, who always got left out because everyone thought he was weird. Nelle reminded her friends that she wasn't afraid of Sonny. In fact, one day she stood at the edge of the Boleware yard and chatted with Sonny as he sat on the front porch.

Several days before the party, Sheriff Farrish stopped by the Faulk household and warned Jennie that troubling rumors were afloat: Truman had invited blacks to the party, and the Ku Klux Klan planned to meet at the nearby elementary schoolyard in protest. The sheriff was worried. He even warned Anna, the half-black woman who lived behind the Faulks, to leave town the evening of the party. Nevertheless, Jennie decided not to cancel.

On Friday, during the middle of the party, Sally Boleware, Sonny's sister, ran into the Faulk house, shouting that the Klan had got a hold of Sonny in the Lees' front yard. Nelle, Truman, and Big Boy shot out the back door and jumped over the hedge that divided the Faulk property from the Lee property. According to Big Boy, there on the Lees' front lawn they saw A. C. calmly walk out in his undershirt: "He waded into the middle of the sheet-covered Klansmen, who had gathered in the middle of the road holding their torches high . . . he came face-to-face with a Klansman wearing a hood with green fringe. This was the Grand Dragon."

A Grand Dragon of the Ku Klux Klan flanked by junior members

There, in the center of the crowd, the Klansmen held captive somebody dressed up as a robot. The robot struggled, but his costume made it impossible to move around freely. When Mr. Lee took off the mask, he saw that it wasn't a black man, as the Klansmen had thought. It was Sonny Boleware, "white as a sheet, with tears streaming down his face." Mr. Lee scolded the Klansmen, who burned their torches out in the dirt and departed.

Another account of this incident, which appeared in the *Monroe Journal* in 1934, reports that A. C. disbanded a Klan gathering but doesn't mention Sonny or the party. Whatever really happened, Nelle saw her father stand up and do the right thing. It was a lesson she wouldn't forget.

An Alabama student in 1936

CHAPTER TWO

School Days, Summer Trouble

Nelle Harper hated school. As her alter-ego Scout commented in *To Kill a Mockingbird*, "I did not believe that twelve years of unrelieved boredom was what the state had in mind for me." She could read better than most of the other kids, and further, her teachers were insufferable and scolded her when she asked impertinent questions.

Much of her education occurred outside of school. Every evening, she crawled into A. C.'s lap as he settled into his chair to read a history book or the *Monroe Journal*. Together, they played a game that boosted Nelle's vocabulary: A. C. thought of a word and told Nelle the total number of letters in the word and one specific letter in the word. With this scant information, she guessed what it was. Nelle also learned a lot through overhearing the details of A. C.'s court cases or Alabama state legislative sessions. Sometimes, she overheard discussions about race relations, which at that age Nelle only vaguely understood had something to do with the history of the South.

After the Civil War ended in 1865, the Confederate States were controlled by the victorious Union Army, and subsequently the U.S. Army, which tried to ensure that freed slaves were allowed to vote, access education, and own land. The war-ravaged South had been left in shambles—farmlands scorched and towns razed. At least 295,000 southern soldiers and civilians died from wounds or disease. The South's great challenge was to rebuild without slavery. This was the Reconstruction era, and many southerners resisted it. Between 1866 and 1870, the Ku Klux Klan—which formed in 1865—sought to eliminate the freed slaves, along with the Republican politicians who supported them. Thousands were killed in just a few years. In Louisiana alone, one thousand blacks were killed shortly before the 1868 presidential elections.

When the U.S. Army left the South in 1877, Reconstruction ended. Local politicians instituted laws—collectively called Jim Crow—that prevented blacks from voting or accessing public facilities and made it difficult for poor whites to vote or own land. Ironically, these laws ruined the agricultural lifestyle and economy that southern politicians sought to preserve—during this era, blacks and poor whites who might have rebuilt local economies and thrived as farmers instead fled the South.

Under Jim Crow, blacks and whites had separate restaurants, bathrooms, stores, theaters, churches, and schools. They traveled in separate railway cars and sat in different seats on buses. Blacks weren't allowed to borrow books from public libraries. Most hospitals didn't allow blacks; those that did treated them in

The "colored" water fountain in a streetcar
terminal during the Jim Crow era

rooms in the basement. Blacks weren't allowed to be
firemen or policemen or store clerks. Black lawyers
weren't allowed to practice in most southern courtrooms.
Since blacks were prevented from registering to vote,
they couldn't serve on juries. Blacks and whites couldn't
marry, and mixed children couldn't inherit their father's
property.

In downtown Monroeville, the restaurants, shops,
banks, and grocers were white-only, so growing
up, Nelle's association with blacks was defined by
employee-employer relationships: The Lees hired black
housemaids; black field hands worked at Big Boy's farm;
townspeople hired black laborers for odd jobs. Nelle's
family, like many southerners in the 1930s, believed the
races should live separately. A. C. taught his children
that racial violence was despicable, and that "Negroes"
should be treated with respect.

Nelle made sense of the complexities of life through reading and writing. A. C. had given her and Truman a black Underwood No. 5 typewriter, and from that day forward, they were professional writers. At first, Nelle was skeptical of the typewriter, as she preferred to tell stories out loud. But Truman loved it. Eventually, they established a system in which they took turns dictating stories while the other typed. They lugged the twenty-five-pound typewriter between their houses. Truman also carried a notebook in which he wrote interesting words and stories, and A. C. had given the boy a pocket dictionary that Truman proceeded to carry around until the covers fell off.

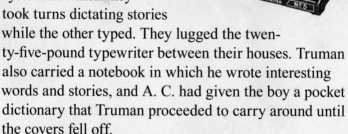

They also engaged in less intellectual pursuits. After Truman moved to New York, he returned to the Faulks' every summer, a time when he and Nelle shot rubber guns, played tag, and caught insects. Nelle was known for her excellence at shooting marbles and climbing tall trees. Another of their pastimes was to watch A. C. during trials at the Monroe County Courthouse. Nelle was in absolute awe of her father. Although A. C. was well-liked by most, some thought him overly proper and emotionally distant. He was a tall man with a stern face who wore dress shoes and a

three-piece suit every day, even when out golfing with friends. He always carried a pocketknife, which he flipped absentmindedly with the air of a preoccupied scholar. On Sundays, when the family attended services at Monroeville Episcopal Methodist Church, he sat in the front row and prayed alone. As a church deacon, he sometimes led the congregation in improvised prayers. In A. C.'s famous editorials at the *Monroe Journal*, he made his opinions known in direct language: he disapproved of drinking, gambling, federal power, inefficient spending, and injustice.

He was, in short, an intellectual with a gentle heart and a quietly stern manner who intimidated some of his peers. As a father, he was loving and affectionate. Nelle later said, "My father is one of the few men I've known who has genuine humility, and it lends him a natural dignity. He has absolutely no ego drive, and so he is one of the most beloved men in this part of the state."

Nelle wasn't as close with her mother, Frances, who suffered what the family called a "nervous disorder." She had trouble sleeping, rarely left the house, and passed many hours sitting silently on the porch swing. A childhood friend of Alice's later recalled that Frances was "very kind and very sweet," but "didn't talk to us at all," and "got up in the morning and started playing that darn piano all day long, or going outside on her front porch and tending to her nasturtiums in flower boxes." She was also known to be a whiz at the *New York Times* crossword puzzle. By the time Nelle was born, her mother's emotional condition had deteriorated as compared to when she was a younger woman, though Nelle later remembered affectionately that her mother read her a story every day.

Frances traveled to Orange County Beach on the Gulf of Mexico every June, attended by A. C.'s secretary. They hoped the weather would improve her nerves. While her mother was away, Nelle spent several summer weeks with her Aunt Alice McKinley—Frances' sister—in Atmore, Alabama. When Frances was home, the task of looking after Nelle was left primarily to the Lees' black housemaid, and also to the community of Monroeville at large, a place where misbehaving children were promptly sent home to their parents. Alice later said in an interview that the Lee siblings were "pretty much allowed to go in the direction we wanted to go, unless we were headed the wrong way."

If Nelle headed the wrong way, it was most likely to occur during the summers, when Truman was in town. One summer, Nelle, Truman, and Big Boy decided they wanted a swimming pool. Aunt Jennie convinced her brother-in-law to dig right in the Faulk side yard. When the small pool was ready, they charged neighborhood kids a nickel each to swim. Nelle recorded each name in a ledger so that if a child went home for dinner, they could return without paying again. Another summer, the three friends organized a carnival that included an exotic catfish and a two-headed chicken that Nelle fashioned together by attaching a dead chicken's head to a live chicken's neck with a wire hanger.

If they couldn't think of something better to do, they told stories. Nelle's favorite destination was the tree house in her back yard, which was filled with old magazines, newspapers, and books. Nelle loved the Hardy Boys series, *Anne of Green Gables*, and the Seckatary Hawkins series. She later recalled with great fondness the stories that her friends told one another, back in the days before prime time television, Wii, and Hulu:

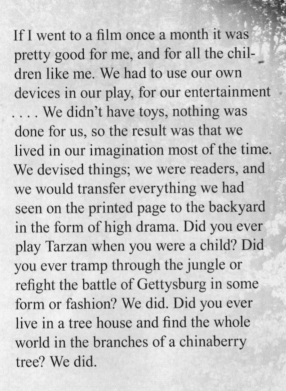

If I went to a film once a month it was pretty good for me, and for all the children like me. We had to use our own devices in our play, for our entertainment . . . . We didn't have toys, nothing was done for us, so the result was that we lived in our imagination most of the time. We devised things; we were readers, and we would transfer everything we had seen on the printed page to the backyard in the form of high drama. Did you ever play Tarzan when you were a child? Did you ever tramp through the jungle or refight the battle of Gettysburg in some form or fashion? We did. Did you ever live in a tree house and find the whole world in the branches of a chinaberry tree? We did.

Nelle grew up during the Great Depression, a time when money was short. In October 1929, the New York Stock Exchange collapsed, and by 1932, the unemployment rate was 25 percent. Workers in industrial jobs, mines, agriculture, and lumbering were especially affected, and since cotton and lumber were big industries in Monroe County, Nelle saw firsthand the farmers who couldn't pay their debts. The southern sharecropping system that emerged after the Civil War was dominated by greedy landowners and poor sharecroppers who squeezed a living from rented patches of land.

A 1932 photograph of a farmer in despair over the depression

The depression ended in 1941, when the U.S. entered the second World War. As a child, Nelle witnessed the end of an agricultural era. Her friends wouldn't grow up to be farmers as their parents had been. Increasingly, large U.S. companies were selling agricultural products abroad. This type of large-scale, industrialized production required machines and financial investments that small farmers didn't have. In 1930, 21 percent of Americans worked in agriculture; in 1970, this was down to 4 percent.

Nelle wrote in *To Kill a Mockingbird* that during the depression, "There was no hurry, for there was nowhere to go, nothing to buy and no money to buy it with, nothing to see outside the boundaries of Maycomb county."

> "There was no hurry, for there was nowhere to go, nothing to buy and no money to buy it with, nothing to see outside the boundaries of Maycomb county."

Itinerant hobos traveled from town to town, looking for work in manufacturing or as field hands. Shantytowns, called "Hoovervilles" after President Hoover, appeared. Hobos knocked on back doors, looking for food or work. Families farmed their own food; even townspeople in Monroeville raised their own chickens. Those who still had jobs suffered wage cuts, so they couldn't buy much.

Truman, however, received elaborate gifts from mysterious sources. One summer, he arrived in Monroeville with a big, green Trimotor Ford toy airplane, claiming he won it in a contest at the New Orleans airport. Nelle and Big Boy coveted the airplane desperately. One day, they stole it and proceeded to fly it off the Faulks' barn roof with Big Boy sitting in the pilot seat. He crash-landed in a hog pen, amidst two large, angry hogs. As Big Boy later remembered, Nelle tried to save his life:

"The Hogs'll get you and eat you alive!" I turned and looked up to see her hold her nose and leap off the barn. She splashed down, sending a wave of nasty, muddy water over the two of us as she landed atop one of the detached, floating wings. We blubbered and sputtered. Nelle grabbed my arm. "Hurry! You gotta get out! *We* gotta get out," she yelled.

Another time, it was Big Boy and Truman who saved Nelle. One afternoon, they journeyed the one-hour walk from Monroeville to Big Boy's farm, picking dewberries along the way. The dusty country road was flanked by open pastures and fields of cotton and corn. Big Boy's mother—Truman's aunt Mary Ida Carter—greeted them, as she often did, with fried sowbelly, grits, eggs, biscuits, and milk. After they ate, Nelle wanted to ride Pal, the family's bay horse. At that time in her life, Nelle had a morbid fascination with pestering animals, and Pal didn't appreciate it when she jabbed him in the side with a stick. In protest, he chomped down on her head and wouldn't let go. Years later, Big Boy recounted what Pal did next:

Then he reared back, pulling Nelle to her tiptoes.
She was screaming and crying, "Help! Help!
My scalp's comin' off!" Truman grabbed her
overalls, dug his heels into the sand, and pulled
as hard as he could, but he was pulling against a
furious thousand-pound horse.

After several whacks from Big Boy, Pal dropped
Nelle. "My head's bleeding!" she cried. Big Boy
and Truman examined her and determined she
hadn't sustained any wounds.

Adventures within the Lee household were less
dangerous. When Nelle was ten, her older sister, Louise, was to be married the day after Christmas. Nelle
wanted a bicycle for Christmas, but she was convinced
that everybody forgot her, as they were engrossed in
Louise's wedding. She went to every store in town, ask-
ing if someone in her family had purchased a bicycle.
At every store, the answer was "No." Nelle couldn't
believe this betrayal. "Nobody's having a Christmas except Wheezy. She's getting a husband," she complained
bitterly. But on Christmas morning, there was a bicycle
under the tree.

As Nelle grew into her preteen years, her aggressive
personality collided with social expectations of young
womanhood. Big Boy remembered that they grew apart:
"She was still a great ally at school because she hit un-
erringly with her fist and without flinching. We boys
respected this, but we'd begun to do things as a group,
and we didn't want Nelle along when we were chas-
ing girls." During these confusing teenaged times, she
dreamed of being a writer. When she was eleven, she
published a poem, "Springtime," in the *Monroe Journal*.
She wouldn't publish again for many years, but as Nelle
matured, her identity as a writer solidified.

A poster encouraging women to work during World War II

CHAPTER THREE

Identity Crisis

Nelle started at Monroe County High School in 1940. During her sophomore year, Miss Gladys Watson, a young woman who lived across the street from the Lees, became her English teacher. As a neighbor, Miss Watson was noted for her gardening and quilting acumen. As a teacher, she was both loved and feared: "I adored her," Sue Philipp, an old friend of Nelle's, would recall decades later. "She gave you two grades. One was for your grammar in a paper—and you got a whole letter taken off for any mistake, and that included commas." Miss Gladys captivated her students by reading plays, books, and poems out loud.

The same year that Nelle acquired Miss Gladys, life in Monroeville changed. On December 7, 1941, the Japanese bombed Pearl Harbor, and the United States declared war. Unlike the Vietnam War and the wars in Iraq and Afghanistan, public opinion wasn't divided over World War II. Everybody wanted to fight Hitler—Germany, Italy, and Japan had forged a powerful partnership know as the Axis alliance. Until the U.S. joined the war, it was actually two separate wars: One was the German assault on Europe; the other was the Second Sino-Japanese War, which began in 1937 when the Empire of Japan invaded the Republic of China. After Pearl Harbor, the European and Asian wars merged into the deadliest war in history. Between 50 and 78 million were killed, including 26 million Russians. Other nations that lost a significant percentage of its population include China, Poland, Greece, Germany, Hungary, Japan, Lithuania, Romania, and Singapore.

The wreckage of the USS *West Virginia* after Pearl Harbor was attacked by the Japanese in 1941

The United States was lucky in that the war itself was fought on foreign land. U.S. citizens banded together to create weapons for its allies, and the Lee household did its part. Edwin left college and served in England and France as a statistical officer for the Air Force's Mustang group. Alice volunteered with the Red Cross; A. C. organized war bond drives. Many young men in Monroeville were drafted, but Nelle's schoolmates were too young to serve, so she wasn't as affected by the war as her older siblings.

During high school, it became evident that Nelle wasn't interested in flirting or getting dressed up like many of the other girls. She still saw Truman over the summers and was friends with Big Boy at school, but she didn't usually join their teenaged adventures. She spent a lot of time at the library. She became quieter and didn't speak much in class, though she developed a quick wit and a biting sarcasm. As a teenager, she simply didn't fit in. She didn't usually play sports with the boys anymore, and she wasn't part of the girls' gossipy dating world. She did her own thing and looked forward to leaving Monroeville.

In 1944, Nelle began attending Huntington College, a selective institution in Montgomery with professors from the great Ivy Leagues up north. The school was situated on a breathtaking, fifty-eight-acre campus. It was a private, Methodist establishment. Students were required to attend chapel every morning. Girls wore a dress, hat, gloves, and heeled shoes when they left campus—which they did frequently, often to flirt with the young men at nearby Maxwell Airfield, where Nelle's brother Edwin was part of the Air Corps. Formal dances between Maxwell and Huntington were frequent.

As a freshman, Nelle was assigned a room with
two roommates in Massey Hall. Each hall had a
"housemother"—a member of the faculty who looked
after the girls. A freshman wasn't allowed to leave in a
car with a boy, and she had to be home by ten-thirty.

Nelle didn't get along with her roommates, who
found her to be strange and off-putting. By this time,
the nonconformist, intelligent, imaginative Nelle had
grown into a young woman of eighteen with a distinc-
tive personality. She chain-smoked, cussed, and told
jokes that her peers didn't understand. She was tall,
with a solid, vaguely masculine build. Later, one of the
young women on Nelle's hall put it this way:

> We were taught that if you had to resort to ugly
> words, you had a very weak vocabulary and
> needed further English study. Actually we were
> not sure what a lot of bad words meant. We were
> ladies in every sense . . . at least, most of us
> were. So, a girl who used foul language was a
> misfit in every sense of the word. Nobody want-
> ed to be around her.

The girls gossiped about Nelle's appearance. She
rarely wore makeup or curled her hair. She wore jeans,
white Bermuda shorts, plain tops, and a brown leather
bombardier's jacket that Edwin had given her. Her big
brown eyes were not accentuated with mascara. She
preferred to cut her brown hair short. She usually avoid-
ed gussying up and skipped the monthly formal din-
ners. She was a bit of a loner, though classmates recall
her volleyball prowess, enthusiastic humor, and love
for one-on-one conversations. "I can still see her telling
wonderful stories with a cigarette dangling from her
lips," one schoolmate, Tina Rood, later remembered.

Nelle was a terrible insomniac. She sat out in the hallway at night, because her roommates went to bed at eleven, and she didn't want to disturb them. That winter, a terrible tornado ripped through Montgomery, and in the aftermath, one of Nelle's hall mates was too scared to sleep, so Nelle offered to keep her company.

During this first year of college, her affinity for writing and literature was apparent. She contributed occasional articles to the *Huntress,* the campus newspaper, and two of her short stories appeared in the Huntington literary magazine, *Prelude.* Her interest in racial matters surfaced. One of her stories, *Nightmare,* is about a girl who hears talk about a lynching: "Best hangin' I've seen in twenty years," the terrified girl overhears.

For her sophomore year, Nelle transferred to the University of Alabama in Tuscaloosa, a campus of 7,500 a few hours from Monroeville. She made an immediate effort to socialize by joining the Chi Omega sorority in the fall of 1945, just as World War II ended and the culture at universities across the nation transformed.

FRATERNITY ROW, UNIVERSITY OF ALABAMA, TUSCALOOSA, ALA.—6

A postcard of fraternity row at the University of Alabama, Tuscaloosa, circa 1943

The veterans who returned to college were older and more jaded than the boys who hadn't served. Having spent their college years at war, many were in their late twenties and ready to start a family. According to one of Nelle's schoolmates, this new batch of men "weren't interested in fraternities, but most were interested in dating and getting an education, in that order, and were serious about both subjects." The famous baby boom began as couples married and had children during college or shortly after.

Once again, Nelle didn't fit in. She didn't date. She disliked Duke Ellington and other popular big band musicians. Her sorority sisters remember her as a loner who didn't talk much, although she was respected for her athleticism, wit, and smarts, and one Chi Omega later said Nelle could be "amiable and funny, too . . . but she was not going to bounce up to somebody and go, 'Hiya, I'm *Nail!*'"

There was another group that Nelle discovered. Upon arriving on campus, she hastened to the offices of the *Crimson White*, the university's newspaper. They didn't have any positions open, so instead Nelle wrote for the *Rammer Jammer*, the school's quarterly humor magazine. The summer after her sophomore year, she commenced "Caustic Comment," a regular column for the *Crimson White* that showcased her talent for parody and political satire.

At the beginning of her junior year, Nelle was appointed editor in chief of the *Rammer Jammer*. She edited the magazine and managed its staff of sixteen. That same year, she enrolled in law school as part of an accelerated program that allowed undergraduates to begin law studies. Many at the University held Nelle in awe. Accustomed to feeling out of place, she was probably unaware of how deeply she was admired. A front-page article at the *Crimson White* paints a detailed picture of Nelle-the-editor:

In case you've seen an intellectual looking young lady cruising down University avenue toward Pug's dressed in tan, laden with law books, sleepy and in a hurry and wondered who she is--she's Nelle Harper Lee.

Miss Lee is editor of the Rammer Jammer (if you've never heard of the Rammer Jammer, it's not Miss Lee's fault), a law student, a Chi Omega, a writer, a Triangle member, a chain smoker, and a witty conversationalist.

She is a traditional and impressive figure as she strides down the corridor of New Hall at all hours attired in men's green striped pajamas. Quite frequently, she passes out candy to unsuspecting freshman; when she emerges from their rooms they have subscribed to the Rammer Jammer.

Her Utopia is a land with the culture of England and the government of Russia; her idea of heaven is a place where diligent law students and writers ascend after death and can stay up forever without Benzedrine.

Wild about football, she played center on the fourth grade team in Monroeville, her hometown. Her favorite person is her sister "Bear."

Lawyer Lee will spend her future in Monroeville. As for literary aspirations she says, "I shall probably write a book some day. They all do."

At the end of her junior year, Nelle stepped down as
editor of the *Rammer Jammer* and traveled to Monroeville. In June, Edwin, now twenty-seven, married Sara
Anne McCall, Nelle's childhood friend and schoolmate.
Nelle was a bridesmaid. Also in June, A. C. and Alice
sold their family's share of the *Monroe Journal*. In
1929, Alice had returned from college to join her dad as
owner of the paper. In 1937, when she was twenty-six,
Alice left Monroeville and worked as a clerk for the IRS
in Birmingham. Soon afterward, a partner in A. C.'s
law firm died, and A. C. saw an opportunity to turn the
firm into a Lee family establishment. Alice enrolled in
law school in Birmingham. In 1943, she passed the bar,
joined A. C.'s firm, and thereafter became one of the
most respected lawyers in Alabama.

A. C. wanted Nelle to join the family law practice.
He probably hoped she would join the *Monroe Journal*
as well. His selling the paper that June implies Nelle
had confessed her growing doubts about becoming a
lawyer.

In August, Nelle returned to the University of Alabama. She was in a highly selective, competitive program with fewer than a dozen female students. During
this fourth year of college, Nelle was even quieter than
usual, rarely speaking to her classmates. She wasn't
sure this incredibly demanding program was something
she even wanted. She had adventure on her mind.

On April 29, 1948, the *Monroe Journal* reported that
Nelle was accepted as an exchange student at Oxford
University. At this time, college exchange programs
were uncommon. They became popular only after
World War II, when Americans formed transatlantic
friendships with their European allies. Student exchange programs were supported by a piece of legisla-
tion passed by Congress in 1948, so Nelle was truly at

The examination halls at
Oxford University in England

the vanguard when she departed for the Oxford summer program in June 1948.

Alice later said that Nelle "fell in love with England." How could she not? She had admired English authors since she was little, and the majestic Oxford campus was a gathering ground for the leading intellectuals and writers of the day. When she returned to Alabama that fall, Nelle attended school for another semester and then called it quits, just one semester short of a law degree. This bold decision meant she wouldn't even receive her bachelor's, since she had started law school her junior year and thus never took the bachelor's exams.

Nelle was about to make a change. Her old friend Truman had proven it's possible to be a professional writer. His first novel, *Other Voices, Other Rooms,* was published in 1948. A review at the *Chicago Tribune* deemed it "as dazzling a phenomenon as has burst on the literary scene in the last ten years." Truman used Nelle as inspiration for Idabel Tompkins, one of the novel's main characters, who emulates Nelle's combination of gender nonconformity, softness, and spunk:

Truman Capote in 1948

"Son," she said, and spit between her fingers, "what you got in your britches is no news to me, and no concern of mine: hell, I've fooled around with nobody but boys since the first grade. I never think like I'm a girl, you've got to remember that or we can never be friends." For all its bravado, she made this declaration with a special and compelling innocence.

Nelle's new plan seemed extreme to her family in Alabama. She wasn't becoming a lawyer. Instead, she was moving to New York City, where she would become a writer.

The New York City skyline in 1950

CHAPTER FOUR

New York City

When Nelle left Alabama, she was twenty-three years old. Her father wasn't thrilled with her decision, but on the other hand, A. C., now almost seventy, believed in making one's own way, so long as it was honorable. So he packed his black Chevy with Nelle's belongings and drove twenty-four miles to the railroad depot in Evergreen. Nelle boarded a train to New York, where Truman was the only person she knew well.

She moved into an apartment at 1539 York Avenue on the Upper East Side of Manhattan, seven blocks from Central Park. The neighborhood was populated by German and Eastern European immigrant families. Outside Nelle's window, children played in the streets, and a lively crowd of store owners and street merchants sold meat, coffee, newspapers, and fresh produce. Her small apartment didn't have hot running water, and she cooked simple meals on a hot plate. In the nighttime, she drank coffee, smoked, and worked on her writing. She crafted a desk by placing a big, detached door onto two wooden sawhorses. She wrote first drafts in longhand and used a one-finger pecking technique to type them out.

Nelle worked at a bookstore when she first arrived in the city, and in 1950, she took a job as a ticket agent for Eastern Airlines. Soon after, she became a reservations clerk for British Overseas Air Corporation. These jobs paid decent money and allowed her to support herself as she worked on her stories. Nelle later observed, "People who write for reward by way of recognition or monetary gain don't know what they're doing. They're in the category of those who write; they are not writers."

She had been in New York for two years when disaster struck. On June 2, 1951, Nelle's mother Frances, whose health had been declining for years, died. Six weeks later, Edwin died suddenly of a brain aneurism at the age of thirty. This was a devastating blow to the family. That spring, Edwin had been called into Air Force service because the Korean War loomed. He was at Maxwell Air Force Base in Montgomery, awaiting news about his possible deployment, when he died in his sleep. He had a three-year-old daughter, Mary, and a nine-month-old son, Edwin Jr., with his wife Sara. At this time, Nelle's sister Louise had an eleven-year-old son; she and her husband Hank Connor lived two hours from Monroeville, in Eufaula, Alabama.

A. C. was seventy-one years old. Within two months, he lost his wife and only son. Edwin had lived in Monroeville, so when Sara and the kids relocated, Alice and A. C. became the only family there. It saddened Nelle to live so far away at such a difficult time, but she didn't return home. She was determined to become a writer, and with Edwin gone, Monroeville wasn't the same. The Lees sold their house on South Alabama Avenue, and A. C. and Alice moved into a brick ranch house nearby. During Christmas, Nelle often couldn't get time off work to travel home. She later reflected on the homesickness that she experienced at this time in her life:

What I really missed was a memory, an old memory of people long since gone, of my grandparents' house bursting with cousins, smilax, and holly. I missed the sound of hunting boots, the sudden open-door gusts of chilly air that cut through the aroma of pine needles and oyster dressing. I missed my brother's night-before-Christmas mask of rectitude and my father's bumblebee bass moaning "Joy to the World." . . . Christmas to me was only a memory of old loves and empty rooms, something I buried with the past that underwent a vague, aching resurrection every year.

As a young woman in New York, Nelle hoped to find a new family of friends. In the early '50s, Manhattan replaced Paris as the cultural capital of the world. The '50s are usually associated with housewives and hula hoops, but it was also a time of cultural transformation. The devastation of World War II, the clashing of cultures, and the power of the atom bomb created parallel, perhaps contradictory desires for technological innovation and world harmony. Cars, dishwashers, and refrigerators defined new levels of consumerism. Automobiles in particular were influential: suddenly, folks could live in one town but work in another. Close-knit communities like Monroeville were replaced with suburbs and strip malls. It was a brave new world.

An original 1950s advertisement in an American consumer magazine for the KitchenAid dishwasher

So "Everything"

So Easy...

Yes, *KitchenAid* is amazingly easy to operate. The front opening door and independently sliding racks mean you load and unload tableware the easiest way. No racks to lift out . . . no "long reaching" . . . no maneuvering! You just load it . . . latch the door . . . press the switch . . . leave it.

Artists and intellectuals felt a creative energy. At Columbia University, the first of the "Beat Generation" writers—Jack Kerouac and Allen Ginsberg—became friends. Andy Warhol, who would become the definitive visual artist of the 1950s, arrived in New York in 1949, the same year as Nelle. Manhattan was becoming an eclectic wonderland for a new generation of writers and artists, who socialized at basement bars and coffeehouses, or in one another's apartments, where they stayed up all night dancing and listening to jazz.

PEEL SLOWLY AND SEE

Andy Warhol

An Andy Warhol design for the 1967 *Velvet Underground* album cover. Warhol, now known for his revolutionary visual art, moved to New York the same year as Nelle.

Nelle, however, was no partier. She didn't fit with the wild group of artists that Truman consorted with, many of whom did drugs heavily and experimented sexually. Nelle wasn't a teetotaler, but she was irritated with the trendy art scene. She didn't care about dressing in the latest fashions or befriending famous artists. She was the type to have a small circle of close friends rather than a large circle of acquaintances. Dr. Grady Nunn, the son-in-law of Nelle's future book editor, recalled a time in 1958 when he and Nelle attended the same party: "She arrived, was introduced around, and then promptly disappeared. I discovered her later sitting on the back steps with our daughter, who was then five."

And yet, Nelle was celebrated at smaller gatherings. She charmed with her warm smile and clever repartees. Ruth Waller, a friend of Nelle's in New York, put it this way: "Nelle Lee is no ordinary person. She is an icono-clast. She had an innate hatred of 'phoniness' and she made no bones about those she liked (who were few) and those she loathed (who were legion). She was one of the most honest and straight-forward persons I ever knew, in a city not noted for those virtues."

In the fall of '56, Nelle had reason to hope her time in New York would pay off. Her friend Michael Brown, a Broadway composer and lyricist, recommended that she show her writing to Annie Laurie Williams, a tal-ent agent. The week after Thanksgiving, Nelle arrived at the agency offices in Midtown with five of her best short stories. "I walked around the block three times before I could muster the courage to go in and give the stories to an agent," Nelle later said. "At the time, I was very shy. Finally, I rushed in, left the manuscripts with the secretary, and left. I prayed for a quick death, and forgot about it."

As it turned out, Annie Laurie Williams special-
ized in selling film and dramatic rights for books, plays,
and musicals. She wasn't the correct person for a new
writer, but her husband, Maurice Crain, was a literary agent. They worked in the same office. Annie, a
diminutive woman of four foot ten, had "a mind like a
steel trap," as novelist Howard Fast later wrote. In 1936,
she convinced Margaret Mitchell, author of *Gone With
the Wind*, to sell the film rights to her book. Maurice
was known for his fastidious organizational skills. He
wasted no time in business but loved the outdoors and
spent many hours gardening. Annie and Maurice had a
house together in Riverton, Connecticut—the Old Stone
House—which later became a getaway for Nelle.

After Maurice read Nelle's submissions, he invited
her to dinner and explained that the stories were good,
but short stories don't sell. She should write a novel instead. Maurice encouraged her to reconnect with him
after she did more work. Nelle felt both elated and mis-
erable—on the one hand, Maurice's comments were an
encouragement, but on the other, it's not easy to write
a novel, and she worked full-time as an airline reservations clerk. Money was tight.

That Christmas Eve, Nelle celebrated with Michael
Brown, his wife, Joy, and their two young sons. The
Browns' large, two-story townhouse was a wonderful place to visit. It felt like a second home. Nelle later
wrote, "Common interests as well as love drew me to
them: an endless flow of reading material circulated
amongst us; we took pleasure in the same theatre, films,
music; we laughed at the same things, and we laughed
so much in those days."

That night, Nelle slept at the Browns' apartment, and
on Christmas morning, one of their sons woke her by
kneading her face. Sleepily, she went downstairs, where

the boys eagerly opened their gifts. The adults watched in amusement. As time went on, Nelle began to wonder if the Browns had bought her a gift. Finally, Joy said, "We haven't forgotten you. Look at the tree."

Sure enough, Nelle spotted an envelope nestled amongst the branches of the Christmas tree. She opened it. Inside was a note: "You have one year off from your job to write whatever you please. Merry Christmas." Included with the note was a blank check. Nelle couldn't believe it. The Browns offered to pay for her rent, food, and everything else for a full year so she could write. Nelle protested that they were out of their minds. They were taking a great risk. As Nelle later wrote in "Christmas to Me," an essay for *McCalls*, Michael's response was firm:

> My friend looked around his living room, at his boys, half buried under a pile of bright Christmas wrapping paper. His eyes sparkled as they met his wife's, and they exchanged a glance of what seemed to me insufferable smugness. Then he looked at me and said softly; "No, honey. It's not a risk. It's a sure thing."

Nelle decided their gift was "Not given me by an act of generosity, but by an act of love." She wouldn't let them down. In January, she appeared at Maurice's office with a new short story and the first fifty pages of a novel, *Go Set a Watchman*. She turned in more and more pages until the end of February, and in May 1957, after a couple of months of editing, they decided the novel was ready to send to publishing companies. They sent it under the title *Atticus*. Meanwhile, Nelle gave Crain one hundred and eleven pages of a second novel, *The Long Goodbye*.

Soon, all thoughts of a second novel disappeared. J. B. Lippincott, a publishing company, wanted to meet with Nelle about *Atticus*. Years later, Tay Hohoff, who would become Nelle's editor and friend, vividly remembered this first meeting: "On a hot day in June, 1957, a dark-haired, dark-eyed young woman walked shyly into our office on Fifth Avenue to meet most of our editorial staff. They were all men, except me, and apparently we looked formidable."

This group explained that *Atticus* was "more of a series of anecdotes than a fully conceived novel." They wanted to see rewrites before buying the book; Nelle worked on it all summer. In October, Lippincott bought the book, but the work wasn't complete. For the next two and a half years, Nelle and Tay worked on edits. The feeling that Nelle's work was a series of short stories rather than a cohesive novel persisted. Tay later wrote, "There were dangling threads of plot, there was a lack of unity—a beginning, middle, and end that was inherent in the beginning." Nelle wrote several drafts. This was before computers, so rewriting was a laborious process. If she was dissatisfied with a particular sentence, she couldn't simply delete it. She had to retype the entire page.

One winter night, Nelle became so frustrated that she opened the window in her apartment and hurled the novel out into the snow. Panicking, she called Tay and confessed; calmly, Tay instructed her to go outside and pick up each page, one by one. Finally, in the spring of 1959, the final draft, now called *To Kill a Mockingbird,* was ready. Before turning it in, Nelle gave it to Miss Gladys Watson (now Watson-Burkett), her high school English teacher, for final edits.

Lippincott told Nelle that the book wouldn't be released for another year. She could spend time on a new project, and sure enough, an exciting offer came her way. By now, Nelle had lived in New York for ten years, and during this time, Truman became rather famous— indeed, he was an active member of the country's intelligentsia. They were still friends, but Nelle was busy with her book and Truman traveled frequently, so they saw one another intermittently. But now, Truman wanted help on a big story. *The New Yorker* had hired him to write an article about a murder investigation about which he was fascinated. In November, a family of four had been brutally murdered in Holcomb, Kansas, a small town of 270 inhabitants.

The crime was enigmatic: each member of the family was found shot dead in different rooms of their house. There were no suspects, and nothing had been stolen. The victims were Herbert Clutter, a wealthy farmer, his wife, Bonnie Clutter, their sixteen-year-old daughter, Nancy, and their fifteen-year-old son, Kenyon. The Clutter family were prestigious members of their community, and Truman wanted to investigate the psychological impact of an unsolved murder case on a small, rural town.

The farmhouse where, in 1959, wheat farmer Herbert Clutter, his wife, and two teenage children were murdered

Nelle was hired as Truman's "assistant researchist," a funny term that he invented. In early December, 1959, they embarked on the journey to Kansas. They caught a train at Grand Central Terminal in New York, rode eighteen hours to Chicago, switched trains, traveled to St. Louis, switched trains again, and proceeded to Manhattan, Kansas, where they disembarked, rented a Chevy, and drove four hundred miles to Garden City, Kansas, just outside Holcomb.

The drive to Garden City was both fearful and exciting. The radio buzzed with an ominous plea about the Clutter murders: "Police authorities, continuing their investigation of the tragic Clutter slaying, have requested that anyone with pertinent information please contact the sheriff's office." Just like when they were kids, Nelle and Truman had embarked on an adventure—and this one was scary.

The friends booked adjoining rooms at the Warren Hotel in Garden City and immediately started interviewing the people of Holcomb. It wasn't easy. Everyone was frightened. Holcomb was, quite literally, in the middle of nowhere. This is how Truman described it in *In Cold Blood*, the book that resulted from this adventure with Nelle:

> The village of Holcomb stands on the high
> wheat plains of western Kansas, a lonesome
> area that other Kansans call "out there." . . . The
> land is flat, and the views are awesomely ex-
> tensive; horses, herds of cattle, a white cluster
> of grain elevators rising as gracefully as Greek
> temples are visible long before a traveler reach-
> es them. . . . After rain, or when snowfalls thaw,
> the streets, unnamed, unshaded, unpaved, turn
> from the thickest dust into the direst mud.

Truman Capote stands in the living room
of the Clutter farmhouse.

The Clutter murders had rendered this isolated community paranoid. "It looked as if the case would never be solved," Nelle later said. "Everyone was looking at his neighbors, wondering if they could be the murderers . . . You'd see porch lights on all night." Two mysterious New Yorkers were not welcomed. Capote in particular turned people off. He strutted about in a sheepskin coat, a long scarf, and moccasins. He was short—five foot four—and his mannerisms were effeminate. He was an open homosexual. Nelle later observed, "Those people had never seen anyone like Truman—he was like someone coming off the moon."

Alvin "Al" Dewey, the Kansas Bureau of Investigation detective assigned to the Clutter case, later recalled, "If Capote came on as something of a shocker, she (Nelle) was there to absorb the shock." It was Nelle who broke the ice in Kansas. She and Truman were invited to a Christmas party. Alvin and his wife, Marie, were in attendance, and everyone got along with Nelle so well that they gave Capote the benefit of the doubt. "After you talked to her for three minutes, you felt like you'd known her for years," Dolores Hope, who was at that party, later said. "She was 'just folks'—interested in others, kind, and humorous."

Having befriended Al, Nelle and Truman had access to the inner workings of the investigation. On December 30, they were at the Deweys' for dinner when Al found out two suspects had been arrested in Las Vegas: Richard Hickock and Perry Smith. These were the guys who did it. Floyd Wells, a convict in the Kansas State Penitentiary, told police that he once worked as a farmhand for the Clutter family. When he and Hickock were cellmates in prison, Hickock became convinced that the Clutters had a lot of cash in their safe. He had told Wells that he and his friend, Perry Smith, would rob the place. When Wells heard about the murders, he contacted the authorities.

Nelle and Truman stayed in Kansas until January 16, 1960. By that time, Smith and Hickock were in custody, and Nelle and Truman interviewed them extensively. Nelle helped convince Al to allow them access to transcripts from the interrogation of Smith, during which he confessed to the crime. After discovering the Clutter safe was empty, Smith had impulsively attacked Herbert and then proceeded to kill the entire family. In the end, Smith took responsibility for all four killings, though it was probably Hickock who shot Bonnie and Nancy.

Richard Hickock collapses seconds after he admitted to the quadruple, shotgun murder of the Clutter family, along with suspect Perry Smith.

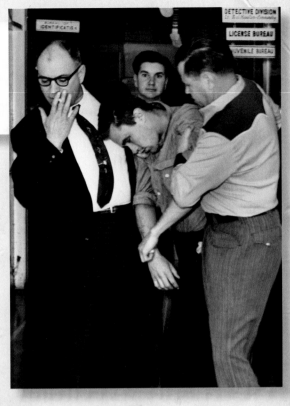

In March, Nelle and Truman returned to Kansas for the murder trial, where Smith and Hickock were sentenced to hang. After Nelle returned to New York, she presented Truman with 150 pages of typed notes based on their time in Kansas, divided neatly into sections like "the crime" and "other members of the Clutter family." By this time, Truman had decided to write a nonfiction book about the murders. The book, *In Cold Blood*, published in 1966, is considered one of the best pieces of journalism ever written. Most are unaware of the extent to which Nelle was involved in the reporting.

Although Truman's ongoing involvement with the Clutter story would be a part of Nelle's life for several years—Truman maintained a relationship with Smith and Hickock until they were executed in 1965—Nelle was distracted with a book of her own. *To Kill a Mockingbird* was published in July 1960, and her life would never be the same.

Nelle with child actress Mary Badham, who played Scout in the film *To Kill a Mockingbird*

CHAPTER FIVE

Mockingbird Flies

Even before *To Kill a Mockingbird* was published, Nelle had reason to suspect it might be successful. In the late winter of 1960, her publicist sent out advance copies to reviewers, with a note stating, "We are rushing this paperbound copy to you so that you may share with us the rare fun and lift in the discovery of a new, fresh talent." Early reviewers were impressed that the copy included a blurb from Truman Capote, who wrote, "Someone rare has written this very fine first novel, a writer with the liveliest sense of life, and the warmest, most authentic humor." The book was selected as recommended reading by both Readers Digest Condensed Books and the Literary Guild, two important honors that often resulted in best sellers.

Folks in Monroeville eagerly anticipated Nelle's debut. She had decided upon the pen name "Harper Lee" because she hated when people called her "Nellie." An ecstatic article in the *Monroe Journal* stated, "Everybody, but everybody, is looking forward to publication . . . of Nell (*sic*) Harper Lee's book, *To Kill a Mockingbird*." Truman was excited, too. In June, he wrote to

friends, "Lippincott is publishing a delightful book: TO KILL A MOCKINGBIRD by Harper Lee. Get it. It's going to be a great success. In it, I am the character called 'Dill'—the author being a childhood friend."

On July 11, 1960, the day finally arrived. Nelle was nervous. She was uncomfortable in the spotlight, where everybody could judge her. She didn't write because she wanted attention; she wrote because she loved it. She later said that when *To Kill a Mockingbird* was published, she was "hoping for a quick and merciful death at the hands of reviewers, but at the same time I sort of hoped that maybe someone would like it enough to give me encouragement."

Within a few weeks, *To Kill a Mockingbird* was a *New York Times* best seller. It stayed on the best-seller's list for eighty-eight weeks. Most critics wrote glowing reviews. *The New Yorker* raved, "Miss Lee is a skilled and totally unpretentious writer who slides unconcernedly and irresistibly back and forth between being sentimental, tough, melodramatic, acute, and funny in this story." Herbert Mitgang at the *New York Times* wrote, "Here is a storyteller justifying the novel as a form that transcends time and place." Another *New York Times* reviewer wrote, "Maycomb has its share of eccentrics and evil-doers, but Miss Lee has not tried to satisfy the current lust for morbid, grotesque tales of Southern depravity." This alludes to popular spin-offs of southern literary masters like William Faulkner, Flannery O'Connor, and Tennessee Williams, whose work reflects the dark underbelly and existential crises of southern society.

To Kill a Mockingbird takes place in the invented town of Maycomb, Alabama, between 1932 and 1935. At its beginning, it's summertime in Maycomb, and six-year-old Scout adventures with her older brother Jem and best friend Dill. They're fascinated by Boo Radley, a recluse who lives in a ramshackle house down the street. As Scout grows older, her father, Atticus Finch, teaches her to control her temper—she's prone to fighting—and practice tolerance. Scout is judgmental of those different than her, including her annoying cousin Frances, Boo Radley, farm kids from the country like Walter Cunningham, and Mrs. Dubose, the mean old lady who lives down the street. But Atticus tells Scout, "You never really understand a person until you consider things from his point of view—until you climb into his skin and walk around in it."

Rural Alabama in 1941

Atticus becomes the defense attorney for Tom Robinson, a black man accused of raping Mayella Ewell, a young white woman. Before the trial begins, an angry mob threatens to lynch Tom, but Atticus bravely protects him and is unexpectedly rescued by Scout. During the trial, Atticus uncovers compelling evidence that Tom is innocent; Mayella and her father had accused him falsely. Nevertheless, the all-white jury finds Tom guilty and sentences him to death. Though Atticus plans to appeal the case, Tom tries to escape from prison and is shot dead by guards. Months later, Scout and Jem are viciously attacked by Bob Ewell, Mayella's father, who is angry that Atticus humiliated him in court. Boo saves Jem and Scout, killing Bob with a kitchen knife in the process. By the book's conclusion, nine-year-old Scout has learned that the law doesn't always protect the innocent. And yet, the brave actions of those like Atticus help ensure the balance of life be tipped toward righteousness.

Some critics found problems with *Mockingbird*'s narrative perspective. *The Atlantic Monthly* reviewer wrote, "It is frankly and completely impossible, being told in the first person by a six-year-old girl with the prose style of a well-educated adult." The same review deemed *Mockingbird* "pleasant, undemanding reading" that is "sugar-water served with humor."

Others thought the Boo Radley and Tom Robinson sections seemed as if part of two different books; the narrative threads didn't fuse together smoothly. Still, most who pointed to structural problems thought the book was good overall.

Nelle wasn't prepared for this amount of attention. For several months, she stayed in New York, meeting with journalists and answering telephone calls. In September, she traveled to Alabama for book signings. A. C., now eighty-one, came along. Suddenly, his daughter was a star and so was he. The character Atticus Finch wasn't a direct translation of A. C., but Nelle admitted the two are alike in "disposition." Friends jokingly called A. C. "Atticus." One reporter commented that Nelle's book "is written out of Harper Lee's love for the South and Monroeville, but it is also the story of a father's love for his children, and the love they gave in return."

A. C. stuck to his characteristic modesty, downplaying comparisons with Atticus and remaining calm about his daughter's success. He told a reporter for *Life* magazine: "I feel what I think a justifiable measure of pride in her accomplishment, and I must say she had displayed much determination, confidence, and ambition to give up a good job in New York and take a chance at writing a book. I'm very proud to be the father of Nelle, and although she has been inclined to write since childhood, I am simply amazed that this thing should happen to her."

From the beginning, *To Kill a Mockingbird* was tied in the minds of its readers to the civil rights movement. Although the book is set in the 1930s, the unjust legal trial of Tom Robinson was relevant to the civil rights era of the '50s and '60s. The juxtaposition of the book's 1960 release with the progression of national affairs was deeply symbolic.

In 1954, the U.S. Supreme Court contested segregation with its *Brown v. Board of Education of Topeka* ruling, which ruled that state laws establishing separate public schools for blacks and whites are unconstitutional, because "separate educational facilities are inherently unequal." This contradicted an older Supreme Court decision that legalized segregation in the first place: *Plessy v. Ferguson* (1896), which determined that state laws requiring racial segregation in public facilities *is* constitutional, public facilities being "separate but equal."

Black communities were more likely to be impoverished and receive less funding from tax dollars, so black-only public facilities were never "equal." The education system was the most conspicuous example: black schools weren't given enough money to purchase basic supplies like books and paper, and students who excelled in these subpar schools weren't allowed to attend prominent state universities in the South, which were for whites only. It was extremely difficult for black individuals to receive an education. Thanks to *Plessy v. Ferguson*, this was the law of the land.

The new *Brown* ruling meant that segregationist laws weren't supported by the federal government. The ruling applied to schools specifically, but it was harnessed to fight other types of segregation. Supreme Court decisions are powerful because they establish legal precedent, meaning that judges in state courts use federal Supreme Court decisions to guide their decisions. If a black student sued a school for barring attendance in 1953, a state judge could argue that white-only schools are constitutional because of *Plessy v. Ferguson*. If that same student sued in '55, after the *Brown* ruling, local judges had to follow a new federal precedent. Nevertheless, the Supreme Court does not have the power to directly force its rulings into effect. This is what happened during the civil rights era, when local battles put new court rulings to the test.

In 1955, Rosa Parks, a civil rights activist, refused to give up her seat on a public bus in Montgomery, Alabama. According to local law, a black person paid for a ticket at the front of the bus, exited, and reentered at the back. If this black section was full, a black person had to stand, even if there were open seats in the white section. If the white section was full, every black person in the row closest to the front vacated their seats so the white person could sit. When Rosa Parks was ordered to leave her seat for a white man, she refused, and was consequently arrested.

Rosa Parks with Dr. Martin Luther King Jr. in the background, circa 1955

This marked the beginning of the Montgomery Bus Boycott, led by Dr. Martin Luther King Jr. The boycott lasted 381 days; Alabama became the center of the burgeoning civil rights movement. On December 20, 1956, a city ordinance ended the segregation of buses in Montgomery. These changes didn't come easily. In '56 and '57, black churches and homes of civil rights leaders in Montgomery were bombed.

In the years that these events unfolded, Nelle wrote the short stories that became *To Kill a Mockingbird.* Several incidents struck close to home. In 1956, Autherine Lucy, a black woman, registered at the white-only University of Alabama in Tuscaloosa, where Nelle had attended college only six years previously. Three nights of mob violence ensued. This occurred contemporaneously to the bus boycott, leading an Associated Press journalist to declare on March 3, 1956, that "the time of racial crisis is now" in Alabama. The article reported that the Alabama legislature sought to banish all blacks from Alabama:

> The Alabama legislature now has pending before it a resolution to seek federal funds to transplant Negroes from the state to places outside the region where they are "needed or wanted." This resolution is indicative of the developing pressures in the Legislature for action against those who would disturb the traditional segregation laws and customs.

Into this tense racial atmosphere, *To Kill a Mockingbird* entered: a book by a white, Alabamian author that protested racial injustice within the U.S. court system through its depiction of the Tom Robinson trial. The book was popular in its own right, but something was about to happen that drastically increased the visibility of Nelle's story.

In 1961, Annie Laurie Williams sold the film rights of *To Kill a Mockingbird*, which would be directed by Robert Mulligan and produced by Alan J. Pakula. The producers asked Nelle if she wanted to write the screenplay; she graciously declined, so they hired Horton Foote, a southern writer. Nelle promptly visited Foote at his home in Nyack, New York—they became "instant cousins" and remained lifelong friends.

That November, the film's art director, Henry Bumstead, visited Monroeville, which he planned to use as inspiration for the Maycomb he would build on-set in Hollywood. In a letter to Alan Pakula, Bumstead wrote, "Harper Lee was there to meet me, and she is a most charming person. She insisted I call her Nelle—feel like I've known her for years." Nelle had many suggestions. She said a block of ice should sit outside the courthouse, because in the days before air conditioning, folks chipped off a piece before going in to watch the trial. She specified that Mrs. Dubose's house should "have paint that is peeling," while Boo Radley's house should "look like it had never been painted—almost haunted." When Bumstead won the Academy Award for art direction, he said part of it belonged to Harper Lee.

In January 1962, Gregory Peck, a famous movie star who was to play Atticus, visited Monroeville. Up until this time, Monroeville was rather calm about Nelle's success. But when Gregory came to town, "That's when people noticed the book," Jane Ellen Clark, whose mother grew up with Nelle, later remembered. "If Hollywood's gonna make a movie out of this book, then there's something about it that's special. One girl said that Gregory Peck came into the bank and wrote a check. She was so nervous she had a hard time giving him his money."

Later that January, Nelle traveled to Garden City, Kansas, to help Truman continue research for his book. By this time, *To Kill a Mockingbird* had been awarded the 1961 Pulitzer Prize in fiction. In its first year of publication, it sold more than 2.5 million copies. Dolores Hope, a friend of Nelle's in Kansas, later wrote, "My impression of the Pulitzer time is that people who had come to know Truman here in Kansas just had a gut feeling that he would have his nose out of joint about it."

After Kansas, Nelle took the Super Chief train to Los Angeles for the shooting of *To Kill a Mockingbird*. She had reservations about Gregory Peck's suitability for the role of Atticus, but changed her mind when she saw him on set:

> The first glimpse I had of him was when he came out of his dressing room in his Atticus suit. It was the most amazing transformation I had ever seen. A middle-aged man came out. He looked bigger, he looked thicker through the middle. He didn't have an ounce of makeup, just a 1933-type suit with a collar and a vest and a watch and chain. The minute I saw him I knew everything was going to be all right because he was Atticus.

Nelle's Hollywood trip was cut short because her nephew's wife had developed pneumonia, so Nelle traveled to Denver to care for her. When she returned to New York, the onslaught of publicity intensified. *Mockingbird* was about to get even bigger, but soon, its author would recede from the spotlight.

Actor Gregory Peck and
Nelle on the set of *To Kill a
Mockingbird* in 1962

Nelle Harper Lee with her
father, A. C. Lee, in 1961

CHAPTER SIX

Fame and Fortune

On April 15, 1962, A. C. Lee died. He had suffered a heart attack the previous year; between publicity stints, Nelle spent time in Monroeville tending to him. One week after his death, the *Montgomery Advertiser* ran an article that honored A. C. in context of the racial battles embroiling Alabama, imploring southerners to stand up for what is right: "There are many 'likenesses' of Atticus Finch. They are far too silent."

After A. C. died, Nelle decided it was time to write her second novel. She had tried in earnest, but demands from family, friends, and the public pulled her in different directions. She wanted to be polite and accept public life, but the busier she became, the more everyone asked about the next book. In July 1961, on the first anniversary of *Mockingbird*'s publication, she received this note from her agents:

Dear Nelle: Tomorrow is my first birthday and my agents think there should be another book written soon to keep me company. Do you think you can start one before I am another year old? We would be so happy if you would.
– The Mockingbird and Annie Laurie and Maurice Crain

Around this time, Nelle moved into a new apartment on the Upper East Side with her friend Marcia Van Meter. No matter where she went, she couldn't concentrate on writing. In Monroeville, she frequently played golf, hoping to clear her head and be alone. Annie and Maurice often invited her to the Old Stone House in Connecticut, and she intermittently took them up on the offer. In 1960, during the first year of *Mockingbird*'s release, Truman wrote to friends that Nelle "seems to be having some sort of happy nervous-breakdown," and in a letter to Al and Marie Dewey, he wrote, "Poor thing—she is nearly demented: says she gave up trying to answer her 'fan mail' when she received 62 letters in one day."

These stresses were compounded by the extreme fanfare accompanying the theatrical openings of *To Kill a Mockingbird* in early 1963. The film highlighted racial conflicts more than the book: Tom Robinson's trial accounts for 15 percent of the book and 30 percent of the movie. Nelle began a new round of public appearances, making a favorable impression on most everyone she met. After she attended the film's premiere in New York, John Casey, who ran the preview room, wrote to Annie Laurie: "Miss Harper Lee has been in many times helping with the promotion of the picture . . . Harper Lee is such a wonderfully warm and friendly woman that I have had all I could do to keep from giving her a big hug right in public." In a letter to Alice, Annie reported Nelle to be "so tired she could hardly sit," and then detailed her success with journalists:

> Phil Gerard (a press agent) says she talks so well
> before little or big audiences and never stops or
> is halting in what she is saying . . . but when she
> gets through, she always thinks she didn't do

so well . . . And I want to end by saying Nelle will carry on with her two next out of town engagements, as she is what we call a "good trooper."

On April 8, 1963, the night of the Academy Awards, Nelle and Alice watched together at a friend's house in Monroeville. *To Kill a Mockingbird* won three awards: Best Actor (Gregory Peck), Best Art Direction (Henry Bumstead, Alexander Golitzen, Oliver Emert), and Best Adapted Screenplay (Horton Foote). Shortly before the ceremony, Nelle had given Gregory A. C.'s pocket watch, engraved "To Gregory from Harper." He held it up during his acceptance speech, and Nelle cried in happiness. She later wrote, "If the integrity of a film adaptation is measured by the degree to which the novelist's intent is preserved, Mr. Foote's screenplay should be studied as a classic."

Gregory Peck holds the pocket watch of A. C. Lee, given to him by Nelle, the morning after he won Best Actor for his portrayal of Atticus Finch.

That summer, with the hoopla beginning to recede, Nelle returned to New York and spent time at the Old Stone House. Annie Laurie reported that Nelle was "looking fine again"—friends and family had been concerned, observing Nelle's weight gain, fatigue, and propensity for alcohol. Alice had taken over the voluminous paperwork surrounding income from the book and movie, in addition to fielding fan correspondence and lecture requests.

The popularity of the film, in conjunction with its relevance to current events, was making *Mockingbird* a favorite with teachers. Three years after its publication, 8 percent of junior highs and high schools had added it to their reading lists. It was considered a liberal novel, but Nelle distanced her work from the particulars of the civil rights era. In an interview with the *Birmingham Post Herald*, she said:

> My book has a universal theme, it's not a 'racial' novel. It portrays an aspect of civilization. I tried to show the conflict of the human soul—reduced to its simplest terms. It's a novel of man's conscience . . . universal in the sense that it could happen to anybody, anywhere people live together . . . It amuses me that 'Mockingbird' is taken as a dreadfully liberal novel by some of our dinosaurs. It's not liberal or conservative. I just hope it's a good book.

Themes and concepts in *To Kill a Mockingbird* include: the innocence of childhood; the power of education, courage, and love to quell bigotry and violence; justice and tolerance; small town society; southern history and its discontents. As children, Scout, Dill, and

A scene from *To Kill a Mockingbird* with the actors who portrayed Jem, Scout, and Dill

Jem are confused by the contradictions of the adult world. Scout is forced to go to school, yet Atticus says it's okay to "bend the law a little in special cases" when it comes to folks like the Ewells. When Miss Maudie, the Finch's neighbor, tells Scout that some Methodists think it's a sin to spend too much time outside gardening, Scout protests with perplexity, "That ain't right, Miss Maudie," not understanding the incongruities inherent to rigid moral codes.

The citizens of Maycomb abide by a series of overlapping codes of law and morality that often contradict one another. There are the customs of the church, which are used for both good and evil. Tom Robinson's church raises money for his wife and children, yet the church ladies in Aunt Alexandra's missionary circle are elitist and hypocritical. Then there are social codes, which define some folks as better than others based on skin color, wealth, family, vocation, and education. There is the law of Alabama's court system, which is imperfect. Sometimes, one works outside the law, like when Atticus and Sheriff Heck Tate decide against arresting Boo Radley for killing Bob Ewell. On the other hand, it can be evil to work outside the law, as seen with the mob of farmers who sought to attack Tom.

Mockingbird's characters struggle to find a balance between following the rules—which are sometimes unjust—and doing the right thing. When Atticus explains that defending Tom is the right thing to do—that he "couldn't go to church and worship God if I didn't try to help that man"—Scout protests. She says Atticus must be incorrect because most folks in Maycomb say so. Atticus's response is one of the core lessons of the book: "The one thing that doesn't abide by majority rule is a person's conscience."

Atticus believes that humans have innate rights that must be upheld by social institutions. If these institutions fail, individuals have the moral responsibility to do what is right. He prizes learning and order over ignorance and chaos. When the mob comes for Tom, Atticus awaits them holding a book, not a gun. He believes in sacrificing life and limb only in extraordinary circumstances; he's even proud when his children place themselves between him and the mob, despite the danger. He believes individual integrity is more important than social standing. He says to Jem:

The one place where a man ought to get a square deal is in a courtroom, be he any color of the rainbow, but people have a way of carrying their resentments right into a jury box. As you grow older, you'll see white men cheat black men every day of your life, but let me tell you something and don't you forget it—whenever a white man does that to a black man, no matter who he is, how rich he is, or how fine a family he comes from, that man is trash.

Gregory Peck (*center, standing*) in the courtroom scene

Despite these views about justice, *Mockingbird* contains no arguments against segregation, partly because it takes place in the 1930s, and partly because Atticus is a socially moderate conservative, as was A. C. Lee. In fact, A. C. had an unsavory confrontation with Reverend Ray Whatley, an anti-segregation preacher of Monroeville's First Methodist Church. In 1952, Whatley delivered a sermon calling for support of federal programs that would prevent racial employment discrimination. A. C., who was chairman of the church's board, told Whatley to stop preaching social issues. The following year, when Whatley delivered another sermon on race relations, the board fired him. Whatley later became a member of the Montgomery chapter of the Alabama Council on Human Relations with Dr. King.

Later, A. C. changed his position. This spoke to his disposition as an individualistic man—when previous opinions didn't match his conscience, he altered them. As the '50s progressed, anti-black violence reached a climax that disgusted most southerners, regardless of their political affiliations. In 1954, Emmett Till, a fourteen-year-old from Chicago visiting relatives in Mississippi, was brutally murdered by two white men after whistling at a white woman. The murderers went free. Closer to home, in 1959, Monroeville canceled its annual Christmas parade after the Ku Klux Klan threatened to kill black high school students. By 1962, A. C. believed steps should be taken to ensure fairer representation of black voters, telling a reporter, "It's got to be done."

Nelle, like her father, was guided by her own lights in political matters rather than the popular stances of political parties. After the film came out, inquiries about the political implications of *To Kill a Mockingbird* continued, and Nelle fielded questions while maintaining her staple humor, as in these excerpts from a 1963 press junket before a roomful of Chicago reporters:

Reporter: Have you seen the movie?

Miss Lee: Yes, six times.

Reporter: What's going to happen when it's shown in the South?

Miss Lee: I don't know. But I wondered the same thing when the book was published. But the publisher said not to worry, because no one can read down there.

Reporter: One of your sisters is a lawyer. Is she a criminal lawyer?

Miss Lee: She's not a criminal, no.

.....

Reporter: When you wrote the book, did you hold yourself back?

Miss Lee: Well, sir, in the book I tried to give a sense of proportion to life in the South, that there isn't a lynching before every breakfast. I think that Southerners react with the same kind of horror as other people do about the injustice in their land. In Mississippi, people were so revolted about what happened, they were so stunned, I don't think it will happen again.

.....

Reporter: What do you think of the Freedom Riders?

Miss Lee: I don't think this business of getting on buses and flaunting state laws does much of anything. Except getting a lot of publicity, and violence. I think Reverend King and the NAACP are going about it in exactly the right way. The people in the South may not like it, but they respect it.

The Freedom Riders were a group that sought to integrate interstate buses after a Supreme Court ruling outlawed segregation in interstate transportation terminals. The first group left from Washington, D.C., on May 4, 1961. Their bus was attacked and burned, and they were later beaten by a mob in Birmingham. In protest against these events, subsequent freedom rides were organized throughout the South.

By the early '60s, the civil rights movement reached a crescendo. In April '63, Dr. King was arrested in Birmingham; in June, President John F. Kennedy promised to extend civil rights to blacks; in August, Dr. King led the Great March on Washington and delivered his "I have a dream speech." In September, four black girls were murdered in a Birmingham church bombing; in November, Kennedy was assassinated. In January 1964, the twenty-fourth amendment abolished poll taxes, which were a tool to prevent blacks from voting. Poll taxes appeared in southern states after Reconstruction. Voters had to pay in order to vote, and this prevented blacks and also poor whites from voting. Other methods to bar voting—methods of disenfranchisement—included literacy tests and violence.

The Civil Rights Act of 1964 is the capstone of the civil rights era. It outlawed segregation in public and most private spaces. It also authorized the U.S. attorney general to enforce school desegregation and prohibited employer discrimination in hiring practices based on race, color, religion, sex, or national origin. To combat disenfranchisement, it stipulated that voting rules and procedures be applied to all races equally. The Voting Rights Act of 1965 allowed anti-disenfranchisement rules to be enforced, and blacks registered to vote en masse. One hundred years after the abolition of slavery, persons of color were given the same legal rights as whites.

The March on Washington in 1963

As these events unfolded and *Mockingbird* became a celebrated text for civil rights supporters, Nelle struggled to write another novel. In the summer of 1963, she took weekend excursions to the Old Stone House, where she played bridge and scrabble with friends between writing sprints. That October, Alice and Louise visited Nelle, Annie, and Maurice in Connecticut. The three sisters departed together, back to Alabama. The next spring, Nelle returned to New York again, thus establishing a pattern that she continued throughout her life of spending part of the year in New York and part in Monroeville.

In the summer of 1964, Nelle vacationed with the Browns at Fire Island, a New York beach destination. Joy Brown, who was nine months pregnant, had her baby before returning to Manhattan, and Nelle stayed behind to help out. That winter, Nelle was in Monroeville when an accident seriously endangered her writing abilities. According to a January 1965 letter from Truman to Perry Smith, "Nelle is in the hospital, the result of a serious kitchen accident. She burned herself very badly, especially her right hand. It seems some sort of pan caught fire and exploded—all this at her home in Alabama."

The hand was burned so badly that it needed to heal for several months before determining if surgery was required. Unable to write or type and with her hand wrapped in gauze, Nelle gave a talk that March to undergraduates at the U.S. Military Academy at West Point. That summer, with her hand a bit more mobile, she returned to her ongoing battle with the book manuscript. By this time, the press had caught on that Nelle wasn't interested in the spotlight. She routinely turned down interviews and invitations to speak or teach.

In the summer of '65, Nelle returned to Fire Island, hoping the change in scenery would improve her output. In a letter to Alice later that year, Annie wrote with sympathy that Nelle was "depressed when she didn't come back from Fire Island with a finished manuscript." Instead, she returned from Fire Island and was told by her doctor that she needed plastic surgery, as there was enough scar tissue to impair her hand forever. Annie and Maurice took her to the hospital, and then Maurice looked after her as she recovered. Nelle was thirty-nine and single; Annie, Maurice, and the Browns were like her family. There are no accounts of Nelle ever being in a long-term, sexual relationship. Some have theorized she might be bisexual, have trouble with intimacy, or both; Nelle has never commented on these topics.

After her surgery, Nelle and her high school English teacher, Gladys Watson-Burkett, boarded the *Queen Elizabeth* and crossed the Atlantic to spend a month together in England. Then, in the spring of 1966, Nelle was appointed to the National Council on the Arts by President Lyndon Johnson. For six years, Nelle, along with other appointees, was entrusted with selecting which arts organizations, programs, and individuals would receive funding. It was Gregory Peck who recommended Nelle for the post. Fellow member R. Philip Hanes later said: "Gregory just worshipped her. . . . when Harper would walk in, he would jump up like a lightning bolt and pull out her chair."

Nelle settled into a private life, declining most invitations to lecture or teach while maintaining letter correspondence with friends, colleagues, and fans. She remained active as a church member in Monroeville and with local education programs. In '62, she had donated significantly to the First United Methodist Church of Monroeville, and she continues to support them today.

In the mid-'60s, at the request of a friend, she spoke to a creative writing class at Sweet Briar College in Virginia. Her remarks about writing, though truthful and honest, suggested a creeping despair:

> To be a serious writer requires discipline that is iron fisted. It's sitting down and doing it whether you think you have it in you or not. Everyday. Alone. Without interruption. Contrary to what most people think, there is not glamour in writing. In fact, it's heartbreak most of the time.

In 1967, Nelle moved into a new apartment on the Upper East Side, her third residence since moving to New York in 1949. Though wealthy, she lived modestly. In 1968, Maurice Crain became ill with cancer. Nelle became one of his caretakers as Annie struggled to keep the agency running. Maurice died in 1970. Maurice and Nelle had been very close friends, but their thoughts about one another are unknown—Maurice's letters and correspondence are housed today at Columbia University in New York, but any correspondence with Nelle is conspicuously absent.

In the early '70s, Tay Hohoff retired from work, and she passed away in 1974. Annie Laurie Williams passed in 1977. The team that had once awaited Nelle's second novel no longer existed, and Nelle no longer talked about writing one.

WE MARCH TOGETHER
CATHOLIC
JEWS
PROTESTANT
FOR DIGNITY
AND BROTHERHOOD
OF ALL MEN UNDER GOD
NOW!

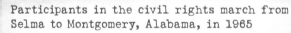

Participants in the civil rights march from
Selma to Montgomery, Alabama, in 1965

CHAPTER SEVEN

The Mockingbird Legacy

In 1976, Nelle Harper, now fifty years old, accompanied Truman to an interview with *People* magazine. Whereas Nelle had disappeared from the public eye, Truman sought it out. The legacy of *To Kill a Mockingbird* was out of Nelle's hands; by the late '70s, it had sold more than 10 million copies. Decades later, Reverend Thomas Lane Butts, pastor emeritus of the First Methodist Church in Monroeville and a longtime friend to Nelle and Alice, reflected that while being famous is fun at first, "I'm quite sure it gets old, when you have people look at you not for who you are but for the image that they have of you."

By eschewing literary fame, Nelle protected herself from this dissonance between private identity and public image—somewhat like Atticus Finch, who was the same in the courtroom as in the public streets. But Truman suffered the effects of celebrity. During the *People* interview, Nelle explained that she and Truman had always been "bound by a common anguish"—the anguish not only of being different from others, but of possessing an intelligence that made them feel apart from the world, looking in as if through a window.

This common anguish no longer sufficed to bind them together. In the late '70s, Truman succumbed to drug and alcohol addiction. Alice later said that Truman had always been jealous of Nelle's Pulitzer. When he started heavily into drugs, "that was it. It was not Nelle Harper dropping him. It was Truman going away from her." Truman had always tested the loyalty of his friends, insecure about their love, terrified of abandonment.

In 1984, Truman died of some ambiguous combination of liver cancer and drug overdose. Nelle attended the memorial service in Los Angeles with Al and Marie Dewey. In 1988, a posthumous biography of Truman quoted him as claiming that Nelle's mother had tried to drown her in the bathtub when Nelle was two. Alice told the *Monroe Journal* that this was "a fabrication of a fabrication . . . My mother was the gentlest of people." In a fuming letter to a friend, Nelle called the story a "vicious lie," concluding that Truman was "paranoid to a terrifying degree. Drugs and alcohol did not cause his insanity, they were the result of it."

Shortly before his death, Truman had his own words about Nelle's drinking habits, claiming that she would drink heavily and then "tell somebody off—that's what it amounted to. . . . People were really quite frightened of her." This might be a Truman-esque exaggeration, but it's true that Nelle went through sporadic periods of heavy drinking, and though she was kind and overly sympathetic by nature, she didn't suffer fools lightly: she said what was on her mind. The little girl who fought in the school yard lived within.

As an older adult, Nelle could be defensive and irritable. Reverend Butts, who remained friends with Nelle and Alice until they were little old ladies, said in an interview that Nelle has "hell and pepper in her . . . She has that public reserve but her feelings get expressed rather graphically sometimes. An injustice stings her to the bone." Comparing Nelle with her sister, Butts said:

Truman Capote in 1959

Miss Alice is very thoughtful and slow moving; very wise in her council and would not take
any risks. She is a good guide. Nelle Harper is
a more impulsive person and more expressive
of her thoughts and ideas. They're both brilliant
people, but they have different temperaments.
Nelle Harper tends to sparkle, whereas Alice is
very quiet and reserved. Nelle Harper loves to
travel and go to the exciting places.

It was this sense of adventure that led Nelle to *The
Reverend*, a book project she started in the '80s. In the
mid-'70s, W. M. "Reverend" Maxwell, a preacher in Alexander City, Alabama, was arrested for killing his wife.
Tom Radney, an attorney, defended him. Maxwell was
found not guilty, and was subsequently tried and found
innocent of the murders of his second wife, brother, and
nephew. Finally, at the funeral of his niece—his fifth
victim—Maxwell was shot dead by one of the niece's
relatives.

With the research support of Radney, Nelle started
a book about these murders. She traveled to Alexander
City and stayed in a hotel as she examined trial records.
For three months, she worked at her sister Louise's
house in Eufaula. But, according to Radney, she never
finished the book, despite calling him with updates on
its progress for several years. In the '80s, Radney said
Nelle is "fighting a battle between the book and a bottle
of scotch. And the scotch is winning." Some theorize
she finished the book and will publish it posthumously.

Even as Nelle's second book remained elusive, her
first was popular as ever. In 1988, *To Kill a Mockingbird* was taught in 74 percent of the nation's public
schools. In 1991, the Monroe County Heritage Museums opened the Monroe County Courthouse as a full-
time museum, and that spring, Monroeville commenced

its annual stage production of *To Kill a Mockingbird*, which still runs today. The first half takes place on the lawn outside the courthouse, and for the second half, audience members go inside for a reproduction of the Tom Robinson trial. During intermission, twelve white male members of the audience are selected to act as the jury. It's an eerie and emotional feeling when the audience members are forced to pass down the terrible verdict: Guilty.

In 2001, Nelle joined with the University of Alabama to sponsor an annual essay contest for high school students on the topic of how the South has or hasn't changed since *Mockingbird* was published. Until recent health problems, Nelle attended the awards ceremony every year, speaking with students while avoiding the press. In 2006, when Nelle was seventy-nine, the *New York Times* reported on the ceremony, describing Nelle as "quick-witted and gregarious." Nelle said that young readers always see "new things" in *Mockingbird*, adding that "the way they relate it to their lives now is really quite incredible."

Nelle applauds as the winner of the *To Kill A Mockingbird* High School Essay Contest is announced on January 23, 2004, in Tuscaloosa, Alabama.

Over time, the public's relationship with the book has changed. Due to its enormous popularity in schools, it ranks on the American Library Association's list of books that are frequently challenged for potential banning. The first famous challenge occurred in 1966, when the Hanover County School Board in Richmond, following a complaint from a local physician, labeled it "improper" and "immoral" due to the rape trial. A flurry of disputes followed, and Nelle wrote to the local paper, expressing incredulity at charges against *Mockingbird*'s morality: "Surely it is plain to the simplest intelligence that 'To Kill a Mockingbird' spells out in words of seldom more than two syllables a code of honor and conduct, Christian in its ethic, that is the heritage of all Southerners."

Hanover wasn't the only district distressed by the rape trial. Earlier charges against the book usually came from conservatives who, amongst other complaints, disliked the depiction of Mayella Ewell, a lewd white woman. Nelle had been influenced by real rape trials of the 1930s. The most famous was the Scottsboro Boys trials. In 1931, two white women alleged that nine teenage "Negroes" had raped them on a freight train. A fast and unfair trial in Scottsboro, Alabama, convicted all nine boys and sentenced eight to death. During the subsequent retrials, it became evident that the rape accusations were false. Over a course of several decades, the Scottsboro Boys were paroled, released, or pardoned.

When Nelle was young, a similar trial occurred in Monroeville. In 1933, a white woman, Naomi Lowery, accused a black man, Walter Lett, of raping her near a brick factory outside Monroeville. Lett was tried by a jury of twelve white men, found guilty, and sentenced to death by electrocution. Many whites in Monroe County thought Lett was falsely accused; they objected so vocally that the governor of Alabama twice delayed the execution. As Lett waited on death row, six black men in his prison were electrocuted. He heard their screams and afterwards suffered a mental breakdown. In 1937, he died of tuberculosis in an insane asylum. In the late '90s, Nelle told a writer that these events had inspired the Tom Robinson trial.

Controversy about miscegenation—the mixing of different racial groups through marriage, cohabitation, sexual relations, and procreation—has been a source of hatred between blacks and whites. Black men were perceived as menacing, lustful creatures who sought to defile white women. One study found that rumors of black men attacking white women sparked 50 percent of race riots between Reconstruction and World War II. Sexual relations between black men and white women were the ultimate taboo.

The Tom Robinson trial was an atypical scenario compared with how allegations against black men usually transpired. Often, they occurred outside the court system. White men attacked blacks suspected of interracial relationships or sexual assaults, often based on rumor and without accusation by a woman. Another scenario occurred when a white woman became pregnant by a black man. She might claim rape to protect herself, her family, and her social standing, sometimes accusing a man she doesn't know in order to protect her real lover. In the fictional case of Mayella, it was her father, Bob Ewell, who made the initial rape accusation. It was Bob who had beaten Mayella, and, as revealed during the trial, he also frequently raped his daughter.

Another dark side to the history of interracial relations is that black women didn't have legal recourse when they were raped, whether by black or white men. During slavery, slave women belonged to their owners.

The birth of mulatto children during slavery is testimony to the relationships between white owners and black women—consensual or otherwise. After slavery, black women were unprotected by the law. In 1892, journalist Ida B. Wells said that as black men were being lynched, "The rape of helpless Negro girls, which began in slavery days, still continues without reproof from church, state, or press."

In 1944, Recy Taylor, a twenty-four-year-old sharecropper in Abbeville, Alabama, was abducted by seven white men with guns and knives, raped by six of them, and then left on the side of the road. Recy immediately went to the white sheriff, who was unconcerned. She then contacted the NAACP in Montgomery, who put their best investigator on the case: Rosa Parks. Though Recy's rapists ultimately went free, the case drew public attention to the plight of black women. Finally, in 1959, an all white jury in Tallahassee, Florida, convicted four white men of raping a black woman at knifepoint. The judge sentenced all four to life in prison. This conviction widened the possibilities for black women to find justice in the U.S. court system.

Tom Robinson's trial in *To Kill a Mockingbird* was relayed by eight-year-old Scout, so its portrayal was relatively tepid. Still, it didn't sit well with many, and beginning in the late '70s, a new wave of challenges was leveled against the book: *To Kill a Mockingbird* was considered racist. Challenges of this nature picked up after 1981, when Warren Township, Indiana, contended the book "represents institutionalized racism under the guise of good literature." In 1985, a similar challenge was supported by the NAACP.

It's true that *Mockingbird* is told from a white perspective and contains one-dimensional black characters. A 1963 *Time* review of the *Mockingbird* film saw

Tom Robinson as portrayed by actor Brock Peters

Tom as the stereotypical "good Negro" who is "just too goody-good to be true." In 1966, critic W. J. Stuckey wrote that Calpurnia, the Finches' housemaid, fills the "lovable 'mammy'" stereotype. Novelist James McBride, in an interview about *Mockingbird* for *Hey, Boo*, a recent documentary about Harper Lee, said that Nelle's perspective as a white writer "doesn't absolve her of the responsibility of handling the character Tom better." Nevertheless, McBride said that when he read *Mockingbird* as a boy, "it was the first time I read a book by a white writer who really discussed the issues of racism in any way that was complicated and sophisticated."

When *Mockingbird* was published in 1960, its contents weren't surprising for many black readers, who lived daily with the fear that friends or family might suffer a fate like Tom's. Rather, the book was illuminating for white readers. Nelle's narrative technique of showing racism through the eyes of a child allowed them to witness certain aspects of their society. Mark Childress, a novelist who grew up in Mississippi, recalled in *Hey, Boo* the impact that *Mockingbird* had on white readers in the '60s:

> It gives white southerners a way to understand the racism that they've been brought up with and to find another way. And for white southerners at that time, there was no other way. There were either outsiders yelling at you because you were a racist cracker, or your leaders, George Wallace saying, "I'll never be out-niggered again." There was no middle ground. Most white people in the South . . . were not throwing bombs and causing havoc, but they had been raised in the system . . . the book really helped them come to understand what was wrong with the system in a way that any number of treatises could never do, because it was popular art, told from a child's point of view.

Historical writer Diane McWhorter, who was a girl in Birmingham, Alabama, when the *Mockingbird* film was released, recalled what it was like to sympathize with Tom Robinson at a time when racial hatred in Birmingham was at its peak: "I started getting really upset about being upset, because by rooting for a black man you were kind of betraying every principle that you had been raised to believe in. And I remember thinking,

Governor George Wallace standing defiantly at a door to
block integration at the University of Alabama in 1963

*What would my father do if he saw me fighting back
these tears when Tom Robinson gets shot?"*

Mockingbird stays forever perched on the brink of
the civil rights era, which Atticus hinted at, telling his
children: "Don't fool yourselves—it's all adding up and
one of these days we're going to pay the bill for it." In
her book, Nelle is ambivalent about southern heritage.
Social and racial snobbery are portrayed as a negative
aspect of southern culture, while bigotry, poor education, and irrational hatred are portrayed as the worst
aspects. At the same time, Nelle treasures the South—
its tight-knit communities, its languid pace of life, its
humor, warmth, and hospitality. In *Mockingbird*, Nelle
hoped to show that there was another route for the
South—a way to nurture its best qualities while smiting
out its worst.

Nelle lived to see the future of race relations in the
United States. Today, the problems of the Jim Crow era
have been displaced with urban poverty. During the
Great Migration of 1910 through 1970, African Americans left the rural South for the urban North, where
they faced new problems: low wages; discriminatory
hiring and housing practices; an absence of family
ties. In a practice known as redlining, banks and other
institutions refused to invest in black individuals, businesses, and communities regardless of economic status,
thus creating segregated urban areas. As early as the
1960s, a reverse migration began, during which blacks
returned to the South due to kinship ties and frustrations in the North. More recently, African Americans
and other minority groups were victims of the subprime
mortgage crisis that contributed to the economic col-
lapse of 2008.

African American communities are still influenced by inequities in the legal system. Today, blacks are more likely than whites to be imprisoned for identical crimes. In California in 2010, blacks were thirteen times more likely to be imprisoned than non-blacks for identical marijuana-related offenses. The high incarceration rates of black males divide families and make it difficult for paroled individuals to vote or find employment.

Nelle's opinions on contemporary social issues are unknown. In a 2002 interview, Alice said both sisters are currently Republicans, and Reverend Butts said Nelle has "pointed observations about the nation," but values her privacy too highly to make public statements. "Overall," Butts said, "I think Nelle Harper is frustrated to see the world grow coarse and obscene and not be able to bring about the resolution to our Southern evils, like [racism]."

To Kill a Mockingbird has sold more than 30 million copies and has been translated into forty languages. During the '60s, it allowed readers to perceive injustices in their land. Today, students are still affected by the book. As Harper Lee once said, there is something "universal" in its message. Scout Finch laid bare what injustice looks like, and when her story is read—anywhere and at any time—the color of injustice is recognized, and so too are its cures: love, knowledge, courage, and tolerance.

Nelle smiles during a ceremony honoring the four
new members of the Alabama Academy of Honor on
August 20, 2007, in Montgomery, Alabama.

CHAPTER EIGHT

A Small World

In 1997, Richard Chalfin, a rare books dealer in Manhattan, received a phone call that changed his life. An old woman called to request *When Rain Clouds Gather*, a novel. As Richard processed the payment, he noticed the last name on the credit card: Lee.

"Any relation to Harper Lee?" he asked.

"That's my best friend," the woman replied, laughing. Richard, realizing he had *the* Harper Lee on the phone, stammered about his love for her book and asked why she never wrote another.

"I said what I had to say," Nelle responded. Then she offered to sign a copy of *Mockingbird* for Richard—a generous offer, because, as they both knew, a signed first edition of *To Kill a Mockingbird* was worth thousands. Richard tracked down a British first edition and an American first edition, and then mailed them to a P.O. box in Alabama. A few weeks later, a sturdy old lady with white hair, sneakers, and a pants suit walked into his office. After handing Richard his books, she smiled, gave him a hug, and departed.

While Nelle is often called a recluse, the truth is she continued to live a perfectly normal life, and she's happy to discuss her book publicly when the circumstances are for education rather than publicity or profit. It's true, however, that she doesn't talk about *Mockingbird* with family and friends. She discusses it with Alice only in relation to finances.

Until 2007, Nelle continued to split her time between Monroeville and New York. In the big city, she went to museums, baseball games (she's a Mets fan), used bookstores, and restaurants. When friends came to visit, she relished in describing the layered history of Manhattan's architecture. She preferred taking buses or the subway to taxis and continued to live in her modest Upper East Side apartment.

In Monroeville, she and Alice lived in the brick ranch house the family had purchased in the '50s. In their older years, the sisters settled into a pattern of attending church on Sundays and eating at the local country club. On Sunday afternoons, they hopped into their Buick and drove into the country, exploring back roads and old buildings. Nelle frequented the Alabama Southern College library, where she talked to children about books. Every December, she and Alice made fruit cakes for their friends. When the tiny, petite Alice became older and required a walker, Nelle drove her to work every day at eight in the morning. They frequented the post office to pick up Nelle's fan letters; Nelle would read most of them and respond to a few.

For many years, the sisters ate lunch every Saturday at David's Catfish House in Monroeville with Reverend Butts and his wife Hilda. Butts and Nelle frequently went fishing at the rural property of close friends—after fishing, they would join their friends for a meal of

catfish, sweet potatoes, and hush puppies. According
to Butts, it's "absolutely untrue" that Nelle is a recluse:
"She's a person who enjoys her privacy like any other
citizen . . . She's open, she loves to be around people . . .
I think she has led a happier life and certainly more con-
tented life because she has chosen how she has related to
the public." Both Alice and Butts are vague about Nelle's
charitable giving, but according to Butts, she has paid
anonymously for many student scholarships.

The citizens of Monroeville protect Nelle from the
journalists who pop around every so often, trying to get
an interview with the famously "reclusive" writer. In
2003, John Humphrey, a commentator for BBC, traveled to Monroeville for a story on *Mockingbird*. He and
his crew arrived at the local country club for lunch right
when Nelle and Alice arrived; nobody pointed them out
to him. George Thomas Jones, a Monroeville resident,
said, "Nelle and her sister walked right by them so close
that they could have reached out and touched her."

Nelle's relationship with the Monroe County Heritage
Museums is less pleasant—she dislikes that her book
and its characters are used for merchandising and profit.
She has never attended their annual stage production of
To Kill a Mockingbird, and when the museum published
a cookbook called "Calpurnia's Cookbook," Nelle protested, and they stopped selling it. Today, Monroeville
tourism brings in about 30,000 visitors annually.

Occasionally, Nelle attends public events to accept
awards. In 2007, she was inducted into the Alabama
Academy of Honor. At the awards ceremony, she spoke
only these words: "It's better to be silent than to be a
fool." Also in 2007, she was awarded the Presidential
Medal of Freedom for her contribution to literature. She
traveled to D.C. with Veronique Peck, Gregory Peck's

President Bush (*right*) escorts Nelle to the stage
where he presented her with the Presidential Medal
of Freedom on November 5, 2007.

wife, but she didn't speak at the ceremony. In 2008, despite poor health, she traveled to Birmingham to accept an
honorary law degree from the Alabama Bar Association.

Nelle's decision to never publish another book is less a
mystery than a convergence of circumstances. First was
the incredible pressure of an astonishingly successful debut. "I'll put it this way," Alice said in a 2002 interview.
"When you have hit the pinnacle, how would you feel
about writing more? Would you feel like you're compet-
ing with yourself?" There were also the frustrations of
publicity. According to Alice, Nelle thought journalists
took "too many liberties with what she said. . . . So she
just wanted out." For someone who hates phoniness, the

literary world is a tough pill to swallow. There was also the sheer stress of traveling around, and during the '60s, personal troubles and a poorly timed hand injury probably made writing overwhelming. At some point, Nelle decided it simply wasn't worth it.

Living to a grand old age in Monroeville may be the most rebellious action ever taken by Nelle Harper, who always had an independent mind and a nonconformist disposition. As small town life disappeared, Nelle stayed in Monroeville. As the world became infiltrated with mass media, Nelle attended local literary events. "It takes a lot of courage that almost nobody has in this country, where celebrity is our religion," novelist Mark Childress said about Nelle. "It's a kind of blasphemy in this society that she commits by refusing to participate in the publicity machine."

In 2006, she even turned down an interview with Oprah—though she did meet with her for lunch in New York. "We were like instant girlfriends," Oprah recalls. "She said to me, 'You know the character Boo Radley?' And she said, 'Well, if you know Boo, then you understand why I wouldn't be doing an interview, because I really am Boo.'"

Since the '60s, Nelle has presented two pieces of published work to the public. Both are nostalgic and critical of contemporary society. In 1983, she presented a paper called "Romance and High Adventure" at the Alabama History and Heritage Festival. She discussed Albert James Pickett, an Alabamian historian who published the *History of Alabama* in 1851, which spanned the European settlement of Alabama up through the defeat of the Creek Indians and Alabama's addition to the Union in 1819. Nelle began the speech with a criticism of modern society:

We Americans like to put our culture into disposable containers. Nowhere is this more evident than in the way we treat our past. We discard villages, towns, even cities, when they grow old . . . these are impatient days; more than ever it seems that we want everything but the real thing: we are afraid that the real thing might be dull, demanding, and worst of all, lacking in suspense.

Nelle said that local histories are inherently suspenseful and that Americans have neglected to educate themselves about the details of their own past. She concludes the speech with a theory about why Pickett's history book ends in 1819:

I think Pickett left his heart at Horseshoe Bend. I do not believe that it was in him to write of the eventual fate of the Creek Nation, of the Cherokees, of the Chickasaws and Choctaws, which was decided well within his lifetime. Pickett's *History of Alabama*, this unique treasure, now lies hidden in old family bookcases, has been discarded by libraries, sometimes turns up in rummage sales, and is certainly not used in our schools.

As an author, Nelle's fate was the opposite of Pickett's. Yet what of her second novel? Did she have the heart to write about race relations and the fate of small towns, which were decided well within her lifetime? Nelle expressed her desire to "leave some record of the kind of life that existed in a very small world." As she grew older, this goal became increasingly anachronistic.

Today, local businesses in Monroeville have been superseded by McDonald's, Walgreens, and Rite Aid. Strip malls line the highway. Nelle's childhood home was torn down and replaced with Mel's Dairy Dream. The site of the Faulk house is an empty lot, and a Conoco station graces the spot where the Boleware house once stood. Ironically, the remnants of small town life exist by virtue of Nelle's book. The Monroe County Courthouse has been carefully restored; it is the headquarters of the Monroe County Heritage Museums, and Mockingbird pilgrims tour the trial room that inspired the story.

"Since the thirties, the town's spread out, that's for sure," said Jane Ellen Clark, former director of the Monroe County Heritage Museums, in a recent interview:

> And on Saturdays, the square's dead, which is very different. People shop elsewhere now. We have a Walmart. The downtown is some lawyers' offices, a few stores, and the post office. But in '35, everything was here.

One thing that didn't change since '35 is Nelle Harper and her typewriters. Until she suffered a stroke in 2007, she continued to peck away at them—one in New York, another in Monroeville. She maintained prolific letter correspondence with friends and the occasional fan or colleague. "Her letters are like a short story," Butts said. "Her powers of description are extraordinary." Friends like to theorize that she continued to write stories on those typewriters.

Into old age, Nelle read voraciously. Her and Alice's home in Monroeville is jammed with books. In 2006, Nelle published a short letter in *O: The Oprah Magazine*, on the topic of stories and books:

> Now . . . in an abundant society where people
> have laptops, cell phones, iPods, and minds
> like empty rooms, I still plod along with books.
> Instant information is not for me. I prefer to
> search library stacks, because when I work to
> learn something, I remember it.

Attorney Alice Lee (*left*), Monroe County Circuit
Judge-elect Dawn Hare (*center*), and Harper Lee (*right*)
share a good laugh in this 2006 photo. Alice Lee
serves as a gatekeeper between the public and Harper.

In her 1964 interview with Roy Newquist, Nelle posited that many of the great American novelists came from the South because southern culture encourages storytelling. "Our whole society is geared to talk rather than do," she said. "Any time spent on business is time more or less wasted, but you have to do it in order to be able to hunt and fish and gossip. . . . Of course, this kind of South is becoming a thing of the past. We're becoming industrialized . . . we're beginning to concentrate in the cities. But it will take quite a while to take the small town out of the South—we're simply a region of storytellers."

Sometime after suffering her stroke, Nelle moved into a residential care facility in Monroeville. Today, at the age of one hundred, Alice still works in her law office above a bank in downtown Monroeville—the same office A. C. worked in. Every afternoon, like clockwork, she visits Nelle, who is eighty-six. Both sisters are nearly deaf, and Nelle has lost 95 percent of her vision. She is still able to read with the assistance of a powerful magnifying machine. Reverend Butts says Nelle has begun to lose her memory when it comes to recent events, but she remembers the past with precision, and loves to sing songs and tell stories. "I have friends who love me and take care of me," Nelle told him recently. "I'm one of the luckiest people in the world."

Gregory Peck, portraying Atticus Finch,
embraces Mary Badham as Scout in a scene from the film.

Timeline

1926 Born Nelle Harper Lee on April 28, in Monroeville, Alabama.

1940 Begins at Monroe County High School.

1944 Leaves home for Huntington College.

1945 Transfers to the University of Alabama at Tuscaloosa.

1946 Becomes editor of *Rammer Jammer*; begins law school.

1949 Drops out of law school; moves to New York City.

1950 Takes job at the British Overseas Air Corporation.

1951 Mother Frances dies on June 2; brother Edwin dies on July 12; Alice and A. C. purchase new house in Monroeville.

1956 Brings short stories to agents Maurice Crain and Annie Laurie Williams.

1957 J. B. Lippincott purchases *To Kill a Mockingbird*.

1959 Travels to Kansas with Truman Capote to report on the Clutter murders.

1960 *To Kill a Mockingbird* published.

1961 *To Kill a Mockingbird* awarded the Pulitzer Prize in Fiction.

1962 Father A. C. Lee dies April 15; *To Kill a Mockingbird* film released.

1965 Burns hand; travels to England with Gladys Watson-Burkett.

1966 Appointed to National Council on the Arts.

1970 Good friend Maurice Crain dies.

1983 Delivers "Romance and High Adventure" speech at the Alabama History and Heritage Festival.

1984 Lifelong friend Truman Capote dies.

1991 Monroe County Courthouse restored, opens as permanent museum; annual *To Kill a Mockingbird* stage adaptation commences there.

2001 Inducted into the Alabama Academy of Honor; starts annual *To Kill a Mockingbird* essay contest with the University of Alabama.

2006 Receives honorary degree from University of Notre Dame; publishes letter in *O: The Oprah Magazine*.

2007 Awarded the Presidential Medal of Freedom at the White House; suffers a stroke that renders her wheelchair-bound.

2012 Lives in residential care facility in Monroeville.

Sources

Chapter One: Carefree In Alabama

p. 11, "There were so many demands . . ." Marja Mills, "To Find a Mockingbird," *Chicago Tribune*, December 28, 2002.

p. 12, "I have about 300 . . ." Charles J. Shields, *Mockingbird: A Portrait of Harper Lee* (New York: St. Martin's Griffin, 2006), 236.

p. 13, "I hope to . . ." Roy Newquist, "Roy Newquist Interview With Harper Lee," *Counterpoint* (Chicago: Rand McNally, 1964), http://www.thebluegrassspecial.com/archive/2010/july10/harper-lee-interview.php.

p. 13, "We were not . . ." Mary McDonagh Murphy, ed., *Scout, Atticus, and Boo: A Celebration of Fifty Years of To Kill a Mockingbird* (New York: HarperCollins, 2010), 121.

p. 15, "most boring place . . ." Shields, *Mockingbird: A Portrait of Harper Lee*, 38.

p. 16, "one of the handsomest . . ." Ibid., 49.

p. 18, "Hot grease in . . ." Ibid., 31.

p. 18, "Get offa him . . ." Ibid.

p. 18, "He wore blue . . ." Harper Lee, *To Kill a Mockingbird* (New York: Harper Perennial, 2006), 8-9.

p. 18, "like a bird . . ." Shields, *Mockingbird: A Portrait of Harper Lee*, 33.

p. 20, "Mr. Boleware ruined . . ." Ibid., 54.

p. 20, "To live in the hearts . . ." Ibid.

p. 20, "absolutely true . . ." Kerry Madden, *Harper Lee: A Twentieth Century Life* (New York: Penguin Group, 2009), 61.

p. 20, "Mrs. Ralls . . . cooked three . . ." Marianne M. Moates and Jennings Faulk Carter, *A Bridge of Childhood: Truman Capote's Southern Years* (New York: Henry Holt and Company, 1989), 117.

p. 22, "He waded into the middle . . ." Ibid., 61-62.

p. 23, "white as a sheet . . ." Ibid., 62.

Chapter Two: School Days, Summer Trouble

p. 25, "I did not believe that twelve . . ." Lee, *To Kill a Mockingbird*, 37.

p. 29, "My father is one . . ." Shields, *Mockingbird: A Portrait of Harper Lee*, 67.

p. 29, "nervous disorder . . ." Mills, "To Find a Mockingbird."

p. 29, "very kind and very sweet . . ." Shields, *Mockingbird: A Portrait of Harper Lee*, 39.

p. 30, "pretty much allowed . . ." Murphy, ed., *Scout, Atticus, and Boo: A Celebration of Fifty Years of To Kill a Mockingbird*, 122.

p. 31, "If I went to a film . . ." Newquist, "Roy Newquist Interview With Harper Lee," *Counterpoint*.

p. 32, "There was no hurry . . ." Lee, *To Kill a Mockingbird*, 6.

p. 33, "The Hogs'll get you . . ." Moates and Carter, *A Bridge of Childhood: Truman Capote's Southern Years*, 104.

p. 35, "Then he reared back . . ." Ibid., 145.

p. 35, "My head's bleeding . . ." Ibid., 146.

p. 35, "Nobody's having a Christmas . . ." Murphy, ed., *Scout, Atticus, and Boo: A Celebration of Fifty Years of To Kill a Mockingbird*, 122.

p. 35, "She was still a great ally . . ." Moates and Carter, *A Bridge of Childhood: Truman Capote's Southern Years*, 150.

Chapter Three: Identity Crisis

p. 37, "I adored her . . ." Shields, *Mockingbird: A Portrait of Harper Lee*, 63.

p. 40, "We were taught that . . ." Ibid., 76.

p. 40, "I can still see her telling . . ." Ibid., 78.

p. 41, "Best hangin' I've seen . . ." Madden, *Harper Lee: A Twentieth Century Life*, 82.

p. 42, "weren't interested in fraternities . . ." Shields, *Mockingbird: A Portrait of Harper Lee*, 83-84.

p. 42, "amiable and funny . . ." Ibid., 86.

p. 43, "In case you've seen . . ." Madden, *Harper Lee: A Twentieth Century Life*, 85-87.

p. 46, "fell in love with England . . ." Marja Mills, "A Life Apart: Harper Lee, the Complex Woman Behind a 'Delicious Mystery,'" *Chicago Tribune*, September 13, 2002, http://articles.chicagotribune.com/2002-09-13/features/0209130001_1_atticus-finch-mockingbird-harper-lee.

p. 46, "as dazzling a phenomenon . . ." Madden, *Harper Lee: A Twentieth Century Life*, 90.

p. 47, "Son," she said, and spit . . ." Shields, *Mockingbird: A Portrait of Harper Lee*, 59.

Chapter Four: New York City

p. 50, "People who write for reward . . ." Newquist, "Roy Newquist Interview With Harper Lee," *Counterpoint*.

p. 51, "What I really missed . . ." Harper Lee, "Christmas to Me," *McCalls*, December 1961, http://web.archive.org/web/20070701015651/http://www.chebucto.ns.ca/culture/HarperLee/christmas.html.

p. 53, "She arrived, was introduced . . ." Shields, *Mockingbird: A Portrait of Harper Lee*, 131.

p. 53, "Nelle Lee is no ordinary . . ." Madden, *Harper Lee: A Twentieth Century Life*, 98-99.

p. 53, "I walked around the block . . ." Shields, *Mockingbird: A Portrait of Harper Lee*, 113.

p. 51, "a mind like a steel . . ." Ibid., 27.

p. 54, "Common interests as well . . ." Harper Lee, "Christmas to Me."

p. 55, "We haven't forgotten . . ." Ibid.

p. 55, "You have one year . . ." Ibid.

p. 55, My friend looked around . . ." Ibid.

p. 55, "Not given me by . . ." Ibid.

p. 56, "On a hot day . . ." Madden, *Harper Lee: A Twentieth Century Life*, 106.

p. 56, "more of a series . . ." Ibid.

p. 56, "There were dangling . . ." Ibid., 109.

p. 58, "Police authorities, continuing . . ." Shields, *Mockingbird: A Portrait of Harper Lee*, 136.

p. 58, "The village of Holcomb . . ." Truman Capote, *In Cold Blood: A True Account of a Multiple Murder and its Consequences* (New York: Vintage International, 1965), 3.

p. 59, "It looked as if . . ." Madden, *Harper Lee: A Twentieth Century Life*, 115.

p. 59, "Those people had never . . ." Ibid.

p. 60, "If Capote came . . ." Shields, *Mockingbird: A Portrait of Harper Lee*, 139.

p. 60, "After you talked . . ." Ibid., 155.

p. 61, "the crime" and "other" . . . Ibid., 180.

Chapter Five: Mockingbird Flies

p. 63, "We are rushing . . ." Shields, *Mockingbird: A Portrait of Harper Lee*, 14.

p. 63, "Someone rare has written . . ." Ibid.

p. 63, "Everybody, but everybody . . ." Ibid., 182.

p. 64, "Lippincott is publishing . . ." Clarke, ed., *Too Brief a Treat: The Letters of Truman Capote*, 284.

p. 64, "hoping for a quick . . ." Newquist, "Roy Newquist Interview With Harper Lee," *Counterpoint.*

p. 64, "Miss Lee is a skilled . . ." Madden, *Harper Lee: A Twentieth Century Life*, 124.

p. 64, "Here is a storyteller . . ." Shields, *Mockingbird: A Portrait of Harper Lee*, 182.

p. 64, "Maycomb has its share . . ." Ibid.

p. 65, "You never really understand . . ." Lee, *To Kill a Mockingbird*, 33.

p. 66, "It is frankly and completely . . ." Phoebe Lou Adams, "*To Kill a Mockingbird*, by Harper Lee," *The Atlantic Monthly*, August 1960, http://www.theatlantic.com/magazine/archive/1960/08/-i-to-kill-a-mockingbird-i-by-harper-lee/6456/.

p. 66, "pleasant, undemanding reading . . ." Ibid.

p. 67, "disposition . . ." Shields, *Mockingbird: A Portrait of Harper Lee*, 215.

p. 67, "is written out of Harper Lee's . . ." Ibid., 185.

p. 67, "I feel what I think a justifiable . . ." Madden, *Harper Lee: A Twentieth Century Life*, 129.

p. 70, "the time of racial crisis . . ." Claudia Durst Johnson, *Understanding To Kill a Mockingbird: A Student Casebook to Issues, Sources, and Historic Documents* (Westport, CT: The Greenwood Press, 1994), 129.

p. 70, "The Alabama legislature . . ." Ibid.

p. 71, "instant cousins . . ." Madden, *Harper Lee: A Twentieth Century Life*, 142.

p. 71, "Harper Lee was there . . ." Ibid., 143.

p. 71, "have paint that is . . ." Ibid., 145.

p. 71, "look like it had never . . ." Ibid.

p. 71, "That's when people noticed . . ." Murphy, ed., *Scout, Atticus, and Boo: A Celebration of Fifty Years of To Kill a Mockingbird*, 93.

p. 72, "My impression of the Pulitzer . . ." Shields, *Mockingbird: A Portrait of Harper Lee*, 209-210.

p. 72, "The first glimpse . . ." Ibid., 213.

Chapter Six: Fame and Fortune

p. 75, "There are many 'likenesses' . . ." Shields, *Mockingbird: A Portrait of Harper Lee*, 215.

p. 75, "Dear Nelle: Tomorrow . . ." Ibid., 202.

p. 76, "seems to be having . . ." Clarke, ed., *Too Brief a Treat: The Letters of Truman Capote*, 292.

p. 76, "Poor thing—she . . ." Ibid., 299.

p. 76, "Miss Harper Lee has been . . ." Shields, *Mockingbird: A Portrait of Harper Lee*, 225-226.

p. 76, "so tired she could . . ." Ibid., 228.

pp. 76-77, "Phil Gerard (a press agent) . . ." Ibid.

p. 77, "To Gregory from Harper . . ." Ibid., 231.

p. 77, "If the integrity . . ." Ibid, 206.

p. 78, "looking fine again . . ." Ibid., 232.

p. 78 "My book has a universal . . ." Madden, *Harper Lee: A Twentieth Century Life*, 127-128.

p. 79, "bend the law . . ." Lee, *To Kill a Mockingbird*, 33.

p. 79, "That ain't right . . ." Ibid., 50.

p. 80, "couldn't go to church . . ." Ibid., 120.

p. 80 "The one thing that . . ." Ibid.

p. 81 "The one place where . . ." Ibid., 252.

p. 82 "It's got to be done . . ." Shields, *Mockingbird: A Portrait of Harper Lee*, 125.

p. 83, "Reporter: Have you seen . . ." Ibid., 221-223.

p. 86, "Nelle is in the hospital . . ." Clarke, ed., *Too Brief a Treat: The Letters of Truman Capote*, 412.

p. 87, "depressed when she . . ." Shields, *Mockingbird: A Portrait of Harper Lee*, 252-253.

p. 88, "Gregory just worshipped . . ." Ibid., 256.

p. 88, "To be a serious . . ." Ibid., 258.

Chapter Seven: The Mockingbird Legacy

p. 91, "I'm quite sure . . ." Murphy, ed., *Scout, Atticus, and Boo: A Celebration of Fifty Years of To Kill a Mockingbird*, 72.

p. 91, "bound by a common . . ." Patricia Burstein, "Tiny, Yes, But a Terror?" *People*, May 10, 1976, http://www.people.com/people/archive/article/0,,20066445,00.html.

p. 92, "that was it . . ." Murphy, ed., *Scout, Atticus, and Boo: A Celebration of Fifty Years of To Kill a Mockingbird*, 127.

p. 92, "a fabrication of . . ." Shields, *Mockingbird: A Portrait of Harper Lee*, 271.

p. 92, "vicious lie. . ." Ibid., 270.

p. 92, "paranoid to a . . ." Ibid.

p. 92, "tell somebody off . . ." Ibid.

p. 92, "hell and pepper . . ." Mills, "A Life Apart: Harper Lee, the Complex Woman Behind a 'Delicious Mystery.'"

p. 94, "Miss Alice is very . . ." Murphy, ed., *Scout, Atticus, and Boo: A Celebration of Fifty Years of To Kill a Mockingbird*, 69-70.

p. 94, "fighting a battle . . ." Shields, *Mockingbird: A Portrait of Harper Lee*, 270.

p. 95, "new things . . . the way," Ginia Bellafante, "Harper Lee, Gregarious for a Day," *New York Times*, January 30, 2006, http://www.nytimes.com/2006/01/30/books/30lee.html?pagewanted=all.

p. 96, "improper . . . immoral," Shields, *Mockingbird: A Portrait of Harper Lee*, 254.

p. 96, "Surely it is plain . . ." Ibid., 255.

p. 98, "The rape of helpless . . ." Danielle L. McGuire, *At the Dark End of the Street: Black Women, Rape, and Resistance—A New History of the Civil Rights Movement from Rosa Parks to the Rise of Black Power* (New York: Vintage, 2010), xviii.

p. 98, "represents institutionalized racism . . ." Valerie Strauss, "Why 'Mockingbird' Has Been Challenged," *Washington Post*, July 11, 2010, http://voices.washingtonpost.com/answer-sheet/literature/why-mockingbird-has-been-chall.html.

p. 99, "good Negro . . ." Alice Hall Petry, ed., *On Harper Lee: Essays and Reflections* (Knoxville, TN: The University of Tennessee Press, 2007), xxxv.

p. 99, "lovable 'mammy' . . ." Ibid.

p. 99, "doesn't absolve her . . ." Murphy, ed., *Scout, Atticus, and Boo: A Celebration of Fifty Years of To Kill a Mockingbird*, 133.

p. 99, "it was the first time . . ." Ibid., 131.

p. 100, "It gives white southerners . . ." Ibid., 78-79.

p. 100, "I started getting . . ." Ibid., 142.

p. 102, "Don't fool yourselves . . ." Lee, *To Kill a Mockingbird,* 252.

p. 103, "pointed observations about . . ." Mills, "A Life Apart: Harper Lee, the Complex Woman Behind a 'Delicious Mystery.'"

p. 103, "Overall, I think Nelle . . ." Ibid.

Chapter Eight: A Small World

p. 105, "Any relation to Harper. . ." Richard Chalfin, "The day Harper Lee Came to See Me," *New York Observer,* December 4, 2000, http://www.observer.com/2000/12/the-day-harper-lee-came-to-see-me/.

p. 105, "I said what I had . . ." Ibid.

p. 107, "Absolutely untrue . . . she's a person," Murphy, ed., *Scout, Atticus, and Boo: A Celebration of Fifty Years of To Kill a Mockingbird,* 71.

p. 107, "Nelle and her sister . . ." Shields, *Mockingbird: A Portrait of Harper Lee,* 276.

p. 107, "It's better to be silent . . ." Madden, *Harper Lee: A Twentieth Century Life,* 176.

p. 108, "I'll put it this way . . ." Mills, "A Life Apart: Harper Lee, the Complex Woman Behind a 'Delicious Mystery.'"

p. 108, "too many liberties . . ." Murphy, ed., *Scout, Atticus, and Boo: A Celebration of Fifty Years of To Kill a Mockingbird,* 128.

p. 109, "It takes a lot . . ." Ibid., 82.

p. 109, "We were like instant . . ." Ibid., 203.

p. 110, "We Americans like to put . . ." Harper Lee, "Romance and High Adventure speech," 1983, Jerry Elijah Brown, ed., *Clearings in the Thicket: An Alabama Humanities Reader* (Macon, GA: Mercer University Press, 1985), http://web.archive.org/web/20070429071626/http://www.chebucto.ns.ca/culture/HarperLee/when.html.

p. 110, "I think Pickett . . ." Ibid.

p. 111, "Since the thirties . . ." Murphy, ed., *Scout, Atticus, and Boo: A Celebration of Fifty Years of To Kill a Mockingbird,* 90.

p. 111, "Her letters are like . . ." Mills, "A Life Apart: Harper Lee, the Complex Woman Behind a 'Delicious Mystery'"

pp. 111-112, "Now . . . in an abundant . . ." Harper Lee, "A Letter from Harper Lee," *O, The Oprah Magazine,* July 1, 2006.

p. 113, "Our whole society . . ." Newquist, "Roy Newquist Interview With Harper Lee," *Counterpoint.*

p. 113, "I have friends who love . . ." Ben Raines, "Alice Lee, Sister of Harper Lee, Like 'Atticus Finch in a Skirt,'" *Press-Register,* June 10, 2011, http://blog.al.com/live/2011/06/alice_lee_sister_of_author_har.html.

Bibliography

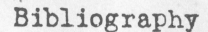

Adams, Phoebe Lou. "*To Kill a Mockingbird*, by Harper Lee." *The Atlantic Monthly*, August 1960. http://www.theatlantic.com/magazine/archive/1960/08/-i-to-kill-a-mockingbird-i-by-harper-lee/6456/.

Bellafante, Ginia. "Harper Lee, Gregarious for a Day." *New York Times*, January 30, 2006. http://www.nytimes.com/2006/01/30/books/30lee.html?pagewanted=all.

Blackford, Holly. *Mockingbird Passing: Closeted Traditions and Sexual Curiosities in Harper Lee's Novel*. Knoxville, TN: The University of Tennessee Press, 2011.

Bloom, Harold, ed. *Modern Critical Interpretations: To Kill a Mockingbird*. Philadelphia, PA: Chelsea House Publishers, 1999.

Bond, Sharon. "The Lasting Call of the Mockingbird." *St. Petersburg Times*, August 13, 1995.

Burstein, Patricia. "Tiny, Yes, But a Terror?" *People*, May 10, 1976. http://www.people.com/people/archive/article/0,,20066445,00.html.

Capote, Truman. *In Cold Blood: A True Account of a Multiple Murder and its Consequences*. New York: Vintage International, 1965.

Chalfin, Richard. "The Day Harper Lee Came to See Me." *New York Observer*, December 4, 2000. http://www.observer.com/2000/12/the-day-harper-lee-came-to-see-me/.

Churcher, Sharon. "Don't Mention the Mockingbird!" *Daily Mail*, June 27, 2010.

Clarke, Gerald, ed. *Too Brief a Treat: The Letters of Truman Capote*. New York: Random House, 2004.

Dimitri, Carolyn, Anne Effland, and Neilson Conklin. "The 20th Century Transformation of U.S. Agriculture and Farm Policy." United States Department of Agriculture, June 2005. http://www.ers.usda.gov/Publications/EIB3/.

Flynt, Wayne. "Still Bright and Bold, an Alabama Treasure Turns 100." *Press-Register*, September 18, 2011. http://blog.al.com/press-register-commentary/2011/09/still_bright_and_bold_an_alaba.html.

Hoffman, Roy. "Long Lives the Mockingbird." *New York Times,* August 8, 1998. http://www.nytimes.com/1998/08/09/books/bookend-long-lives-the-mockingbird.html?pagewanted=all&src=pm.

Johnson, Claudia Durst, ed. *To Kill a Mockingbird: Threatening Boundaries*. New York: Twayne Publishers, 1994.

———. *Understanding To Kill a Mockingbird: A Student Casebook to Issues, Sources, and Historic Documents*. Westport, CT: The Greenwood Press, 1994.

Lee, Harper. *To Kill a Mockingbird*. New York: Harper Perennial, 2006.

——."Love, in Other Words." *Vogue*, April 15, 1961. http://web.archive.org/web/20070630201936/http://www.chebucto.ns.ca/culture/HarperLee/love.html.

——."Christmas to Me." *McCalls*, December 1961. http://web.archive.org/web/20070701015651/http://www.chebucto.ns.ca/culture/HarperLee/christmas.html.

——."When Children Discover America." *McCalls,* August 1965. http://web.archive.org/web/20070429071626/http://www.chebucto.ns.ca/culture/HarperLee/when.html.

——."Romance and High Adventure." 1983 speech, printed in *Clearings in the Thicket: An Alabama Humanities Reader*. Ed. Brown, Jerry Elijah. Macon, GA: Mercer University Press, 1985. http://web.archive.org/web/20070429071626/http://www.chebucto.ns.ca/culture/HarperLee/when.html.

——."A Letter from Harper Lee." *Oprah Magazine*, July 1, 2006.

Madden, Kerry. *Harper Lee: A Twentieth Century Life*. New York: Penguin Group, 2009.

Males, Mike. "Misdemeanor Marijuana Arrests Are Skyrocketing." Center on Juvenile and Criminal Justice, November 2009.

Mancini, Candice, ed. *Racism in Harper Lee's To Kill a Mockingbird*. Farmington Hills: Greenhaven Press, 2008.

McGuire, Danielle L. *At the Dark End of the Street: Black Women, Rape, and Resistance—A New History of the Civil Rights Movement from Rosa Parks to the Rise of Black Power*. New York: Vintage, 2010.

Mills, Marja. "To Find a Mockingbird." *Chicago Tribune*, December 28, 2002.

——. "A Life Apart: Harper Lee, the Complex Woman Behind a 'Delicious Mystery.'" *Chicago Tribune*, September 13, 2002. http://articles.chicagotribune.com/2002-09-13/features/0209130001_1_atticus-finch-mockingbird-harper-lee.

Moates, Marianne M., and Jennings Faulk Carter. *A Bridge of Childhood: Truman Capote's Southern Years*. New York: Henry Holt and Company, 1989.

Murphy, Mary McDonagh, ed. *Scout, Atticus, and Boo: A Celebration of Fifty Years of To Kill a Mockingbird*. New York: HarperCollins, 2010.

Newman, Cathy. "To Catch a Mockingbird." *National Geographic,* January 2006. http://ngm.nationalgeographic.com/ngm/0601/feature8/.

Newquist, Roy. *Counterpoint*. Chicago: Rand McNally, 1964.

Petry, Alice Hall, ed. *On Harper Lee: Essays and Reflections*. Knoxville, TN: The University of Tennessee Press, 2007.

Raines, Ben. "Alice Lee, Sister of Harper Lee, Like 'Atticus Finch in a Skirt.'" *Press-Register*, June 10, 2011. http://blog.al.com/live/2011/06/alice_lee_sister_of_author_har.html.

Schultz, Stanley K. "American History: Civil War to the Present." http://us.history.wisc.edu/hist102/index.html.

Shields, Charles J. *Mockingbird: A Portrait of Harper Lee*. New York: St. Martin's Griffin, 2006.

Strauss, Valerie. "Why 'Mockingbird' Has Been Challenged." *Washington Post*, July 11, 2010. http://voices.washingtonpost.com/answer-sheet/literature/why-mockingbird-has-been-chall.html.

Stoddard, Brooke C., and Daniel P. Murphy. "American Civil War, Casualties." http://www.netplaces.com/american-civil-war/horrors-of-war/casualties.htm.

"Rise of the Ku Klux Klan." *American Experience*, PBS.org. http://www.pbs.org/wgbh/americanexperience/features/general-article/grant-kkk/.

Web sites

http://www.neabigread.org/books/mockingbird/readers02.php

National Endowment for the Arts page on *To Kill a Mockingbird*.

http://web.archive.org/web/20070626182320/http://www.chebucto.ns.ca/culture/HarperLee/index.html:

"To Kill a Mockingbird and Harper Lee," a Web site that features Harper Lee's interviews and published articles.

www.pbs.org/wnet/americanmasters/episodes/harper-lee-hey-boo/watch-the-full-documentary/2049

The PBS documentary *Harper Lee: Hey, Boo* is available for viewing on this site. The documentary "chronicles how this beloved novel came to be written, provides the context and history of the Deep South where it is set, and documents the many ways the novel has changed minds and shaped history. For teachers, students or fans of the classic, *Hey, Boo* enhances the experience of reading *To Kill a Mockingbird*."

Index

Photo Credits

All images used in this book that are not in the public domain are credited in the listing that follows:

1: Courtesy of Ed Morgan

2: Courtesy of Ed Morgan

9: Courtesy of Ed Morgan

10: The George F. Landegger Collection of Alabama Photographs in Carol M. Highsmith's America, Library of Congress, Prints and Photographs Division.

12: Courtesy of Ed Morgan

13: Courtesy of Ninjatacoshell

14: Courtesy of Ed Morgan

15: Courtesy of Library of Congress

16: Courtesy of Ninjatacoshell

17: Courtesy of Library of Congress

19: Courtesy of Ninjatacoshell

20: Courtesy of Library of Congress

21: Courtesy of Ed Morgan

22-23: Courtesy of Library of Congress

24-25: Couresy of Library of Congress

26: Courtesy of Ed Morgan

27: Courtesy of Library of Congress

28 bottom: Courtesy of Minnesota Historical Society

31: Courtesy of Ed Morgan

32: Courtesy of National Archives and Records Administration

33 left: Courtesy of Ninjatacoshell

33 right: Courtesy of Ed Morgan

34: Courtesy of Timur Mamedrzaev

36: Courtesy of Library of Congress

37 top: Courtesy of Ben Towle

38: Courtesy of U.S. Navy

43: Courtesy of Ed Morgan

45: Courtesy of Mike Knell

46: Courtesy of Library of Congress

47: Courtesy of Ben Towle

48-49: Courtesy of Library of Congress

51: Jeff Morgan 13 / Alamy

52: Pictorial Press Ltd / Alamy

57: Bettmann/Corbis / AP Images

59: AP Photo

61: Bettmann/Corbis / AP Images

62: Everett Collection Inc / Alamy

63 top: Courtesy of Ben Towle

64-65: Courtesy of National Archives and Records Administration

66: Courtesy of National Archives and Records Administration

69: Courtesy of National Archives and Records Administration

73: Bettmann/Corbis / AP Images

74: Time & Life Pictures/Getty Images

77: Bettmann/Corbis / AP Images

79: AF archive / Alamy

81: AF archive / Alamy

85: Courtesy of Library of Congress

86-87: Courtesy of Patrick Gruban

90-91: Courtesy of Library of Congress

92-93: Courtesy of Library of Congress

95: AP Photo/The Tuscaloosa News, Robert Sutton, File

99: Moviestore collection Ltd / Alamy

101: Courtesy of Library of Congress

104: AP Photo/Rob Carr

108: AP Photo/Gerald Herbert

112: AP Photo/Kevin Glackmeyer

113: AP Photo

Foliage not listed courtesy of Ed Morgan